You Got This!

Mental Game Skills for Young Softball Players

Dr. Curt Ickes

You Got This!

Mental Game Skills for Young Softball Players

Portions of this book were previously published in *Win the Next Pitch* (2022).

First Paperback Edition: 2022 Published by KDP

Edited by: Olivia Fisher

You Got This!
Mental Game Skills for Young Softball Players

This is a book that teaches important mental game skills to young softball players. These sport psychology skills are usually taught at the high school, college, or professional level. These skills are also life skills, as they can be applied to any performance situation to help curb anxiety and build confidence. At the conclusion of the book, there is a review section to help remember and put into practice the lessons just learned.

In this book, you will follow Ava, Zoe, Addie, and the rest of the Southport Sting as they learn the importance of playing softball one pitch at a time. Zoe has always had trouble getting over errors and bad at bats. But with the help of a new friend, Ava, she learns how to reset quickly using the Three Ts. Zoe also learns the importance of using deep breathing to help control anxiety and anger. Research shows that this type of breathing helps a player gain control over their physical body, which improves performance.

Finally, our young player discovers what a pre-pitch routine is and why it is important to use such a routine before every pitch. This four-step approach helps hitters tune out distractions, so concentration is maximized when they need it most: right before the pitch is made.

Young players will learn:
- **How to play softball one pitch at a time**
- **Skills to sharpen concentration and stay confident under pressure**
- **How to quickly reset after mistakes**
- **What pre-pitch routines are and how to use them correctly**
- **How to use these mental game techniques in other stressful situations like school or other sports**
- **Specific ways to practice these mental game skills off the field so they become automatic during the game**

I hope that reading this book brings pleasure and knowledge, both of which will make playing the game of softball even more enjoyable and fulfilling.

Now, let's meet the Southport Sting!

Table of Contents

1

New Friends

"Whew! I think that's the last one," Ava wheezed as she made it through the front door carrying a large box. Ava's arms screamed in protest as she set it down and slid it next to a stacked mountain of other cardboard boxes.

"Mom! That's the last one," she said looking at her mother. Ava wiped the sweat coating her forehead with the back of her hand. Her chest heaved with exertion, and she placed her hands on her hips, gathering her breath.

Sunlight streamed into the room, catching on the particles of dust floating in the air. Ava brushed the strands of blonde hair from her eyes.

Her mother crouched over a box and cut the tape, pulling out a pile of dinner plates. "Thanks, Ava. Now, we need to unpack. Moving is tough work! Isn't it?"

"Yeah it is. Where is everyone?" Ava asked as she helped her mother unload the rest of the dinner plates from the box. She unwrapped the bubble wrap and stacked the plates on the kitchen counter.

"Your dad and little brother are upstairs putting his bed together. I think Oliver is hiding in the living room somewhere. Maybe you can get him to come out?"

Ava softly walked into the living room scanning as she went. "Where are you, Oliver? Oliver? Come here Oliver." Ava bent down and glanced under the couch. A pair of wide, uncertain, black eyes stared back at her.

"There you are!" Ava smiled and knelt. "Come here, buddy."

"It's okay to be scared. This is all new, isn't it? This move is a big change for everyone. Changes can be scary, but I'm sure we'll be okay, Oliver." Ava petted the big cat on the head, and he crawled out from under the couch and started purring.

She whipped her head around to the sound of thumping footsteps. Her younger brother Luke bounded down the stairs, flying into the living room. "Come see my room! It looks awesome," he hollered, skidding to a stop and grinning. "Ava, come look at it!"

"Okay, okay," Ava said, but before she could follow him, the doorbell rang. Luke sprinted toward the front door and craned his neck to see who was outside on the porch. Ms. Davis put down the dishes she had been washing and wiped her hands on a towel.

"It's a lady and a girl. They're holding something," he announced.

Their mother, still wiping her hands, walked towards the door. Before she got there, Luke flung it open. Oliver darted back under the couch.

A short woman with crow's feet and dark, brown hair pulled into a bun smiled. "I'm Sarah Harris. This is my daughter, Zoe." She nodded her head at the girl next to her. "We live two houses down the street and thought we would welcome you to the neighborhood.

We've brought you coffee and donuts for an energy boost."

"Donuts!" Luke rubbed his hands together and stretched his neck to see inside the cardboard box.

"Hi, I'm Sharon Davis," his mother said, stepping aside and gesturing. "Come on in."

"Yeah, come on in. That's my sister, Ava over there and our cat Oliver is somewhere in there," Luke said pointing into the living room and hopping around.

The two mothers traipsed into the kitchen, talking amongst themselves.

Ava said, "Hi Zoe. Come in here. Do you want to meet Oliver?"

Luke bounded into the living room, giddy with energy. "I've got a hamster in my new bedroom upstairs. Do you want to see it? Do you like snakes? I'm going to get a snake someday. Do you want to go outside and see my bike?" he rambled, barely taking a breath.

Ava frowned. "Why don't you go grab a donut? I bet there's one filled with jelly."

Luke stopped talking, his eyes growing wide. "Bye!" he said suddenly as he raced off to the kitchen. Zoe giggled as Ava rolled her eyes.

"That's just my pesky five-year-old brother," she said.

"I have a little brother, too! Zoe exclaimed. "He's eight. My older sister is fifteen, and I'm eleven. I just finished fifth grade. How old are you and what grade are you in?" Zoe asked, flicking her brown ponytail over his shoulder.

"Same age and same grade," Ava said with a smile. She reached back under the couch for Oliver, who slowly crept out.

Zoe crouched to scratch his ears and frowned. "Where's the rest of his tail?"

"He was a stray and showed up with an injured tail from a fight," Ava said, sitting on the edge of the couch. "He became a bobcat after a trip to the vet."

Zoe rubbed the big cat's head. Oliver purred and turned revealing a grey and black swirl pattern on his side. "Awe, he's so cute! He's brave, too, hanging out with a new person in a new house," Zoe said.

"Yeah, he's a pretty tough cat," Ava said with a smile. "Wanna get a donut with me?" Zoe nodded, and the girls grabbed a donut each from the kitchen before slipping into the backyard. A small, freshly manicured lawn bordered in hedges and flowers.

"Why did you move here?" Zoe asked as they sat on the outdoor furniture.

"My dad's work transferred him from Smithfield to Southport. We found this great house, and luckily, my old friends are only an hour away from here. My mom says I'll make plenty of new friends."

"You will!" Zoe said through a mouthful of donut. "I'll introduce you to my friends. Some of them are coming over to my house today and then we're going to the field to play softball."

Ava's eyes widened in surprise. "I play softball too! Do you play on a team?"

Zoe nodded. "I'm going to be the shortstop for the 11U Southport Sting. I played second base last year and we were pretty good. Most of the team is back. We're going to practice this week since our games start soon." She leaped off the seat and feigned swinging a softball bat. "Are you on a team?"

"I'm not, but I played for the Smithfield Scrappers last year. I'm a third baseman," Ava said with a proud grin.

Zoe's mouth fell open. "No way! Wow. You played for the Scrappers? We never played you, but we were in a few of the same tournaments, and you won all of them!" She shook her head in amazement. "You won the 10U State Tournament, right?"

Ava's cheeks flushed. "We had a great team and coach. It was a fun season."

"So humble," Zoe teased. Her eyes danced with laughter in the midmorning sunlight.

"I'll miss playing this season," Ava said looking at the ground. Her shoulders slumped, and she let out a small sigh.

"I'd miss playing too if I didn't play." Zoe frowned. Suddenly, Zoe's face brightened and her voice lifted. "Hey, play with us! My friend Madison just wrecked her bike and broke her wrist, so we're short a player. Do you want to ask your parents?"

Ava's heart thumped against her chest. "I'd love that. Let me talk to my mom and dad."

Ms. Harris stuck her head outside and waved. "Time to go, Zoe!"

The girls hurried back inside and exchanged their cell phone numbers. Zoe texted Ava the coach's phone number too. "I hope you play with us."

"I'll ask my parents. Hopefully, they'll say yes," Ava said, glancing up from her phone. "It's the Sting, right?"

"That's us!" The girls trudged onto the front lawn and the heat of the sun intensified as it passed its apex in the summer sky. "Let me know about today. Hopefully, I'll see you later. Bye!"

Ava, her mom, and Luke waved to their new neighbors as they headed back down the street.

Suddenly Luke turned to her and bellowed, "Where are you going? I'm going too. Mom, tell her I'm going too."

"Going where?" his mother asked with a puzzled look on her face as they stepped back inside.

"Zoe asked me if I wanted to go the field and play some softball with her and her friends. They play on a travel team together. She also said they are short a player and wondered if I can play with them. They are on the Southport Sting, and she gave me their coach's number. What do you think?" Ava quickly rambled.

Her mother knitted her brows together as she slid two glasses of ice water across to her children. "I'll talk to your dad about the travel team," she said. "And, yes you can go play at the field. Just be careful and take your phone with you."

"Mom, I'm going to the field, too!" Luke said, quickly swallowing his glass of water.

She let out a soft laugh. "No. You're not. You need to clean the jelly off your face and wash those sticky little hands. Then you'll help Dad unpack the rest of your things."

Luke huffed and pouted, balling his fists as he stomped down the hall to the bathroom. "I never get to do anything fun. I'll go to the park next time!"

Ava excitedly texted Zoe and skipped into the living room to grab another box, a wide smile stretching her cheeks.

***

Full of new energy, Ava made great progress unpacking over the next hour.

"Thanks for helping. Now, you better get going. Have fun!" her mother said with a soft smile.

"Great! I'll see you later!" Ava said as she scurried towards the garage and the door slammed behind her. After some searching, she found her partially hidden bat bag in the corner behind some boxes. Jamming the bag with her glove, batting gloves, spikes, some softballs and her favorite bat she couldn't stop smiling. She bid her mom goodbye before heading down the street to Zoe's house. Once there, she saw Zoe in the backyard playing catch with a girl. Another girl stood off to the side swinging a bat.

Zoe's hand shot into the air, and she waved excitedly. "Hi Ava!" Zoe shouted as she stopped throwing. "I want you to meet my friends. I told them you just moved in and hopefully can play with us this year."

"This is Addie LeMasters." Zoe tilted her head toward the slim girl with shoulder length blonde hair who rested the bat over the shoulder. "She plays second and is a great hitter. She will lead off for us. Addie is our techie girl. She is a whiz with computers, apps, webpages, you name it!"

"Welcome to the big city of Southport." Addie shifted her weight and giggled.

"A jokester as well!" Zoe rolled her eyes before pointing to another girl. "This is Sophia Thomas. She's a pitcher and first baseman. She's also our best hitter. Not to mention, she's our school's star athlete in other sports too!"

Sophia, a dark-skinned, curly-haired girl, smiled, staring at Ava's bag. She leaned forward. "Does that say Scrappers?"

Ava's eyes danced with excitement. "Yes! I played for them last year." She slipped her softball cap on and pulled her ponytail through the back.

"Whoa, they're good!" Addie piped up, dropping the head of the bat into the dirt.

"Nobody wanted to play them last year!" Sophia tossed the ball into her gloved hand.

"We might have a shot at beating them this year if Ava joins our team!" Addie swung her bat in slow motion and laughed.

"What did your mom say about joining the team?" Zoe asked, braiding her hair.

"My mom said she'd talk to my dad about it first. I'd love to play with you girls. It would be so much fun." Ava smiled, suddenly feeling not so shy.

Zoe shoved her glove into her black and gold Sting bag before slinging it over her shoulder. "Let's go to the park and hit some."

They all gathered their belongings and headed to the ball field, which was only two streets over. Shadows tossed themselves in haphazard shapes along the sidewalk as the sun dipped towards the horizon. As they walked, Ava looked left and right, trying to absorb all she could from her new surroundings.

Sophia stepped beside Ava as they rounded the street corner. "Zoe said we are all in the same grade. I am sure you'll like our school. Everyone is nice, even the teachers." She pulled her buzzing phone out of her pocket and scanned the screen. "Hey, Lily and Grace are coming to the park."

"We'll have half the team there," Zoe smirked.

The girls made it to the park and headed across the dusty field to put their bat bags in the dugout.

"Hey, Sting girls!" a voice echoed from the other side of the field.

They turned their heads to see two figures bounding across the outfield. It was Lily and Grace. As they reached the infield, Ava could see one girl had mousy red curls gathered into a ponytail, with freckles splattered across her face. The other girl had a few pink streaks dyed into her hair and sported a skinned knee.

"This is my new neighbor, Ava," Zoe said, fitting her hand into her glove. "She played for the Scrappers last year and might be our newest player." Pointing to the red-haired girl, she continued, "Ava, this is Lily. She is our right fielder, and that's Grace who plays left."

"Hi, nice to meet both of you! I'm Ava Davis. I play third and pitch sometimes." The other girls smiled back, and said hello.

Sophia clapped her hands together, smacking a ball into her glove. "Let's get started. I'll pitch. Who wants to hit first?" Sophia called out as she stood by a bucket of softballs in the pitching circle. Grabbing a scuffed yellow softball she smiled and said, "Why don't you hit first, Ava? Since you're the new girl. We usually take about ten swings and then rotate players."

Ava pulled her favorite bat from her bag and swung it back and forth, trying to get loose. Her heart thumped in tandem with the whoosh of her bat slicing through the air. The other girls scattered around the field. Their shadows reached like gangly fingers across the grass. Ava's stomach knotted and her palms were sweaty as she gripped the handle of the bat.

I wonder if I'll be rusty, she thought nervously. *It's been a while since I last played.*

On top of that, this time there were over a half a dozen eyes belonging to strangers expecting her skills to match the superstar team she came from.

Ava drew in a deep, slow breath, exhaled, and glanced at her bat before stepping up to the dusty, marred home plate.

Sophia reared back before pitching the ball right down the middle. Ava swung the bat, and there was a loud ping. The softball soared into the air. It flew way over Grace's head, and she whirled around and gave chase.

"Nice one, Ava!" Sophia cheered, whooping, and clapping her hands together. "Way to rip it. Better back up there, Gracie girl!"

Ava's face flushed with heat, and her fingers tingled with excitement. Maybe she wasn't so rusty after all?

Ava's swings were consistently smooth and solid. She sent softballs slicing through the air in every direction of the park. Line drives, long fly balls, and scorching grounders.

Zoe and Addie exchanged a glance, raising their eyebrows as they watched Ava.

Zoe shook her head in awe, crossing her arms. "She can hit, can't she?"

Addie grinned, bouncing on the balls of her feet. "She sure can. I hope she can join the team! Did you notice before each swing, she did that thing where she took a breath and looked at her bat?"

"Yes! I've seen some of the high school girls do that. I think it helps you focus better. Maybe she can teach us. I could sure use some help with my swing." Zoe said, eyes wide.

Ava lowered the bat on her last swing, panting with both exhaustion and thrill. She had not forgotten how to hit. She dropped her bat by her bag, grabbed her glove, and jogged to third base.

As they continued the practice, the girls noticed something else. If Ava missed a ground ball, she would turn her back to the hitter, take a deep breath, pick up some dirt, and calmly throw it down. Ava would then turn back around, ready for the next pitch. She didn't seem to let her mistake stay with her.

***

After almost two hours, the sun had dipped to the very edge of the horizon, and the exhausted girls

15

decided to call it quits. Ava's muscles ached, and her stomach growled as a reminder that it was dinner time. After gathering their things, they said goodbye, and Ava and Zoe headed home in the same direction.

"Hope you can join the team, Ava!" Addie called over her shoulder, and the other girls parroted their agreement.

"Me too! It was great meeting all of you. Bye!"

Zoe and Ava talked non-stop as they walked home. When they reached Zoe's house, Ava said, "I think your friends are really cool. Thanks for inviting me to play today. It was so fun! It was good to feel like myself again."

"I hope you can play for us," Zoe said as she stepped off the sidewalk and moved towards her front porch.

"I'll let you know what my parents say about it," Ava said, wiping the sweat from her face. Hopefully, it's a yes!"

***

Ava trudged through the garage, her feet dragging. Dropping her bat bag, she peered through the screen door and saw her mom setting the table for dinner.

"Perfect timing," she said to herself as she made her way inside, the smell of pizza wafting over her.

Ava stepped around some empty boxes and plopped in her chair as her mom set some extra napkins on the table. She could feel her mouth watering with each breath she took. She was starving. Oliver rubbed himself against her legs. She petted his head absentmindedly.

"How was softball?" Her dad said as he slid out his chair and took a seat.

"It was great! The girls are very nice, and I was hitting some good ones today. I'm beat! Did mom tell you about me wanting to join their team?"

Her dad glanced over at her mom and softly laughed. "Of course she did, and we think it's a great idea! We'll call the coach tomorrow and get all the details—"

Ava cut off her dad as she jumped up from her chair, cheering and whooping. Ava couldn't believe her ears. Excitement coursed through her. She was going to play softball again!

Hearing the excitement, Luke came bounding out of the bathroom, his hands still dripping with water. "What's going on? What happened?"

"I'm going to play softball with Zoe and her friends. I'm so excited!"

"Oh, is that all? I thought it was something else," he said rolling his eyes and climbing onto his chair.

After dinner, Ava and her mother cleaned up the dishes and Ava texted the good news to Zoe. Zoe was equally excited and said she was going to blast the news to the other girls. She reminded Ava that the Sting's first team practice of the year was in just two days. Even though she was physically wiped out, Ava had problems falling asleep that night. Her excited mind imagined all the fun she was going to have this summer.

2

The Great Mistake Eraser

The sun was shining, and a light breeze swept across the field. The Southport Sting travel team was prepping for another season, this time at the 11U level. Last year, they had won two tournaments and placed in the top three in several others. Full of energy, Ava and Zoe made their way to the Archer Field and jabbered the entire walk to the park.

"Ava! Zoe!" Addie yelled from the outfield as she saw the two walking into the dugout.

"Hi!" Ava called out.

"Hey, Addie! Are you ready to go?" Zoe asked as she tossed her bat bag on the bench.

"You bet. I'm always ready to play ball."

Ava and the other girls chatted excitedly as they waited for the coach.

"I'm glad we got a practice in last weekend. I'm feeling ready," Lily said, grinning.

"Me, too," Grace said shaking her head as she tightened her batting glove and bounced on her feet. "Great to have you on the team, Ava!"

"Thanks!" Ava's eyes narrowed as a broad smile filled her face.

"Hi everyone. I'm Coach Moore," a stocky, muscled woman with a white cap on her head and sunglasses called out. Her skin was leathered from many years spent in the sun on the softball field. "It's great to see all of you here today. Most of you played with us last year, but we have a few fresh faces. Why don't you introduce yourselves and tell us what position you play?"

The coach nodded at Ava and smiled.

Her stomach flipped, but she was determined to be brave. She cleared her throat and rolled her shoulders back. "I'm Ava Davis. I play third base and pitch. Last year, I played for the Smithfield Scrappers, and I just moved to Southport this week."

The girls raised their eyebrows at each other and shared impressed smiles.

"It's great to have you on the team, Ava," one girl said. She had dark hair and wore green flecked shoes. "I'm Emma Lopez. I pitch and play first, same as Sophia."

Ava smiled back and fist-bumped a few of the teammates who were near her. One girl even lurched forward and offered her a hug, despite how sweaty they both were. She smiled and hugged back. Ava instantly felt welcomed. One by one, the other new players introduced themselves to the team and traded high fives and fist bumps. One girl moved into the town last year. Another girl claimed she's played softball since before she could walk. The girls giggled at that.

"Time for fielding practice," Coach Moore said, clapping her hands together. Ava stretched her limbs as she reached third base. Zoe sprinted out to shortstop, her trail kicking up dust.

While Ava was a picture of confidence, Zoe was not. This was going to be Zoe's first year playing shortstop as there wasn't anyone to fill the open spot. Last year, Zoe played second base and often struggled, making more than her share of errors.

"I need to make a good impression today. I need to show them last year's mistakes are behind me and that I can play shortstop. I just have to," she said softly.

Her stomach knotted as she crouched down, hands at the ready for the incoming grounder. She chewed her lip and willed the nerves away. But her heart continued to hammer against her chest. Memories of last year's mistakes billowed across her mind in a frenzy.

Coach Moore hit a two-hopper to shortstop. Zoe launched into action, gritting her teeth as sheer determination coursed through her veins. There was a dull smack. The ball hit the heel of her glove, knocking into her shoulder. She let out a grunt and rubbed her shoulder as heat flooded her face and neck.

"Great! Just great!" She said sourly. Zoe moved back to her position and watched the other infielders scoop up ground balls and throw them flawlessly to first.

Her breath was uneasy, and she hoped she wouldn't miss the next one. She could feel her jaw clench in frustration. The next ground ball skidded her way, hugging the dusty sand. Zoe got in position right in front of it…but came up empty. The ball went through her legs and out into left field.

"What in the world?" Zoe muttered glancing at her glove as if there might be a hole in it. "I'll probably miss every ball hit to me! It's going to be just like last year." Deflated, she smacked her glove on her leg, shook her head, and trudged back to her spot at shortstop.

Coach Moore continued hitting infield practice, and Zoe continued to misplay ball after ball. The infield softballs continued to soar past her, slicing between her legs or bouncing off her glove and body. It was as if the softballs had a magic spell on them and were consciously avoiding her. After each miss, her heart sank a little bit more, and her confidence slipped further away. Zoe's stomach churned, and her eyes stung with impending tears.

I'm the worst player on the team, she thought.

"Okay, time for some batting practice. We'll start with third and work our way around the field.

Everyone gets fifteen cuts. Ava, you're up," the coach said as she headed to the circle to throw.

Ava grabbed her bat and jogged to the plate, beads of sweat on her forehead and lip. Her powerful practice swings sliced through the air with loud whooshes.

Crack! The softball screamed past the infielders like a low flying jet.

"Wow, I wish I could hit like that," Zoe said as she stood by the dugout sliding her helmet on.

"Me too," exclaimed Addie rolling her shoulders. "She can really smash it, can't she? It's our first real practice, and she is already tearing the cover off the ball."

"Yeah!" Zoe said. "Hey, I just got a new bat last night, and hopefully, it has some hits in it! My old bat didn't, that's for sure." Zoe stepped back and took a slow swing.

"Can I see it?" Addie asked

"Sure," Zoe said as she handed the shiny orange bat to Addie.

"This is nice. I bet you can really rip it with this one!" Addie took a few practice swings as she studied the bat closely. "I love this grip and look at that color! It looks like it's on fire." She took a hard swing.

Bam!

Their conversation was interrupted by the sound of another softball crunching off Ava's bat and sailing over the left field fence.

"Great swing!" Coach Moore called out. "Way to hit the softball, Ava!"

"It looks like we have at least one girl who can crush it," Zoe said, her eyes wide.

"That's for sure," Addie said nodding.

It was Zoe's turn to hit, and she grabbed her new bat and confidently stepped to the plate. Coach Moore's first pitch was down the middle. Zoe swung and missed. The next pitch was the same.

"What's going on?" Zoe muttered as she clenched her jaw.

Pitch after pitch, she either missed completely, hit foul balls, or tapped slow rollers to the infield.

"I can't hit! This bat stinks! I'm terrible!" She said shaking her head and kicking some dirt as she tossed her bat to the ground by the dugout and grabbed her glove before heading to shortstop.

When the practice ended, they headed back to the dugout. The other girls' laughter and jokes echoed in Zoe's head. She chewed the inside of her cheek as she packed her bag, trudging out of the dugout in silence.

"What a bad practice. I'm terrible," she muttered, eyes downcast.

"Should we grab an ice cream cone, Zoe?" Ava said, jogging up next to her. "I heard there's an ice cream shop nearby."

A tiny spark of joy bloomed within Zoe. She started to smile. "It's called the Southport Scoop. I could go for some ice cream in this heat!" She let out an exasperated groan and then giggled.

Hoisting their bat bags on their backs, they started the trek. Heat emanated from their skin as they reached their destination. White painted tables and chairs scattered the outdoor vicinity of the shop, and they greedily grabbed their cones from the server and slumped down at the nearest spot.

"What'd you think about practice?" Ava asked, reveling in the taste of the cold ice cream.

Zoe rolled her eyes, hoping her voice wouldn't break. "I was terrible. Once I missed the first grounder, I just knew I was done."

"What do you mean?" Ava asked while licking her now dripping cone.

"It always happens to me. If I make a mistake, I start thinking I am going to make another and then another. I get more nervous and angrier at myself, and it seems to just get worse. Also, I've noticed that if I strike out the first time up to bat in a game, I start thinking I'm probably going to strike out every time! Sure enough, the next at bat isn't any better. I bet you don't do that. You were awesome today! Addie and I saw your hits."

Ava listened with raised eyebrows and then said something very interesting. "I used to do the same thing, but then I learned something very important. The most important pitch in any game is the very next one. You must play softball one pitch at a time. The goal is to win the next pitch!" She paused to lick some dripping ice cream. "You can't think about past mistakes. I learned how to do a reset, and I've played a lot better since then."

"What's a reset?" Zoe asked.

"It's something you learn to do when things aren't going right. Whenever I make an error or have a bad at bat, I hit my reset button. It gets me ready for the very next pitch, and it's a great way to play better right away."

"How does it work? Tell me," Zoe asked, tossing the last bite of ice cream cone into her mouth.

"It's like a video game," Ava said. "When you hit a reset button on a game, it lets you start over at your last save, right?"

Zoe nodded.

"It's the same idea with softball. When you're messing up, you learn to hit *your own* reset button. You start over. Start fresh, so that you can be focused on winning the next pitch."

"How do I reset? What do I have to do?" Zoe asked, eyes wide.

"There's three parts to resetting." She held up her index finger as she slipped back to the ice cream store counter, returning with a scrap of paper and pencil. "I call them the Three Ts."

Ava scribbled something on the paper. Zoe clasped her hands together, waiting patiently.

"Here," Ava said, sliding the paper across the table. "Hold on to this paper so you can remember them."

Zoe glanced at the paper.

The Three Ts
  Take some deep breaths
  Throw away the mistake
  Tell yourself positive things

"Taking deep breaths?" Zoe giggled, shaking her head. "Aren't we already doing that while running around?"

"Yes, but they have to be the right kind of deep breaths. The kind of deep breaths that slow a busy mind. Whenever I made a mistake, my thoughts swirled around my head, my heart raced, and I'd start panting like a dog! Even my muscles tensed."

"That happens to me too!" Zoe blurted out, fidgeting with the paper. "Everything sped up the moment I missed the first ball. Since I was still mad at myself for missing the first one, I wasn't focused on the next one because I was just worrying about missing it. I was out of control."

"It happens to the best of players," Ava said warmly. "We all make mistakes in the game. Learning how to slow everything down is crucial. You can't change the past, but the present moment is in your control. You can decide the outcome. But if you're stressing over something that's already happened, how can you focus on what's going to happen next? So, taking deep breaths helps calm me down so I can win the next pitch."

Ava paused, a big grin spreading across her face and then asked, "Do you know how to breathe?"

"You're funny. Of course, I do! I breathe every day," Zoe said, laughing.

Ava nodded and said, "I will show you a special type of breathing. It's controlled and conscious. I breathe in through my nose, as slow as possible, using my stomach to draw the air in. Not up in my chest and my shoulders never go up while I breathe. That's the key. You'll feel it in your belly button. I hold my breath for a second before blowing it out of my mouth. When I blow out, the stress goes with it. You can think of the nerves as a tiny monster you are trying to blow out of your body. Sometimes, I do two or three of these if I am extra nervous. Do you want to try?"

"Sure!" Zoe said standing up and giving Ava her full attention.

Step 1. Take a Deep Breath

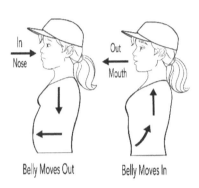

Belly Moves Out   Belly Moves In

They mirrored one another. Zoe followed Ava, drawing in a slow, steady stream of air through her nose until her stomach expanded like a balloon. She held it then blew out the breath through her mouth. The girls took a few more deep breaths. Zoe felt a rush of calm. The racing tornado of thoughts dissipated, and her muscles relaxed.

"What do you think?" Ava asked, staring at her.

"It works great. I feel a lot calmer and more relaxed." A faint, amused smile crossed her face. "What do you do after the deep breaths?"

Ava grinned, letting out a small cheer. "Next, I throw away the mistake. Look, Zoe, every player makes mistakes in softball. It's the nature of the game, and the nature of being a human being, not a robot! But you can't change your mistakes; you can only try to change what will happen next. Skilled players throw away their mistakes. Do you know why?"

"I know! I know!" Zoe said with a huge smile, "Because the most important pitch in a game is the next one! You have to win the next pitch!"

Ava pointed her finger at Zoe like a proud schoolteacher. "Yes! After a mistake, I couldn't stop thinking about it, and I couldn't focus on the next pitch. I ended up playing worse for the rest of the game."

"So, how do you throw away a mistake, especially since it's not something you can hold?" Zoe asked. "I can't help getting mad at my mistakes."

"It's okay to be mad. But you must shake that feeling as quickly as possible."

"I understand. What do you do?"

"You create your own throw away behaviors. They're also called wipe away behaviors. I have different ones depending on if I'm in the field or if I had a bad at bat. If I miss a grounder, I will pick up some dirt or grass, squeeze it tight, and then toss it to the ground. When I throw the dirt down, I tell myself that the bad play went with it, and I forget about it. Look, I'll show you."

Ava pushed her chair back and walked to a patchy section of grass by the ice cream shop. She bent down and scooped up a handful of dirt. "After I take a breath, I'll pick up a handful of dirt, squeeze it tight, and then throw it back to the ground." She squeezed the dirt in her palm and tossed it back to the ground with force.

Step 2. Throw away the mistake

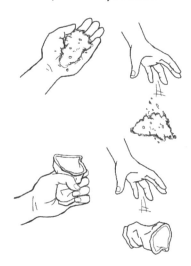

"So, the dirt represents the mistake?" Zoe asked.

"Yes! When I toss the dirt to the ground, I tell myself that the mistake went with it. Then I forget about the mistake!" She motioned her hand over her head. "Poof! Gone! But make sure that it stays away. Don't let it creep back into your thoughts."

Zoe brushed her ponytail behind her head and chewed her lip. "We noticed you did that at the park the other day. That was part of your reset button?"

Ava laughed. "Yep! I have other throw away techniques. Sometimes when I have a bad bat, I will drink from a cup, crush it up, and toss it into the trash.

Other players wipe off their bat. You can do any action, really. Just remember, throwing away means it stays away!"

"I got it," Zoe said. "You actually do something to throw the mistake away, and you are ready for the next pitch. If I'm still thinking about past mistakes, I'm not playing softball one pitch at a time. It hurts my chances to win the most important pitch of the game, the next pitch!"

Ava's face lit up. "Exactly! The last T of the reset is to tell myself positive things. It's called self-talk. You know the voice in your head when you are talking to yourself? Instead of saying mean things to myself after I make a mistake, I tell myself something good. I might say something like, 'You'll get the next one, Ava,' or 'You gave it your best try. You got this.' Yelling at yourself just makes things worse because it makes you feel sad and mad. It also makes you doubt yourself. So, make sure to say something good instead."

Step 3. Tell Yourself Positive Things

"That sounds like something you have to practice," Zoe said, glancing at Ava with a sheepish look.

"Yes, you can get better at it with practice. Remember, being mean to yourself is only going to upset you further. It drains your self-confidence. Turn the negative thoughts into something good."

Zoe shook her head and muttered, "Wow, today at practice I was doing it all wrong. When I was trying to field a grounder, I was still mad and thinking about the ones I missed before. Things just got worse and worse. I missed one ball after another until my confidence was completely gone."

She paused for a moment, sighing. Suddenly, she lifted her head, a wide smile on her face.

"From now on after a bad play or a bad at bat, I am going to take some deep breaths, throw the mistake away, and tell myself something positive," Zoe said. Ava nodded in approval.

***

As they walked home, the girls continued talking softball. They arrived at Zoe's house, and her shoulders loosened with relief. "Thanks for teaching me the Three Ts of resetting. Now I know what to do when I make an error next time. I am going to take some deep breaths, throw away the mistake, and tell myself positive things!"

***

Several days later was the Sting's last practice before the season began. The sun waned in the sky, its burnt orange light bouncing off the aluminum stands, and strands of grass danced in the wispy breeze. There was a frenzy of excitement in the air.

Coach Moore laid some bats out against the fence before carrying a large bucket of balls to the pitching circle. The girls were scattered in the outfield, enthusiastically tossing softballs back and forth as they warmed up for practice. Zoe was playing pitch and catch beside Ava who was throwing with Hannah.

"How's it going, Ava?" Zoe asked scooping up a low throw from Sophia.

"Good! I'm excited for practice today. It should be fun. How are you doing?"

"I'm good. I'm going to try the reset button today," Zoe said throwing her ball to Sophia across from her.

"Definitely try it if you make a mistake today," Ava said, sending her ball in a high arch to Hannah, who snapped it out of the air.

"The past few nights, I've imagined myself on the field after making a mistake. I walked myself through the Three Ts, imagining myself using them. I saw myself doing a great job. I'm sure it will make me a better player in real life. So, if I make a mistake today, I'll try it."

"It works. It'll get easier and easier to use the more you practice it. Let me know if you need help," Ava said with a smile before jogging off.

The Sting then took turns taking batting practice. Ava, once again, was ripping the cover off the ball. Zoe was feeling pretty good about her swings, too. She drilled some solid line drives and even hit a few long balls that almost cleared the outfield fence.

After batting practice was over, Coach Moore had the players take their positions for fielding practice. Zoe pounded her mitt and enthusiastically hustled out to shortstop.

The first ball hit to her was a hard three-bouncer. Zoe scooped it up and fired a perfect strike to first.

"Nice play!" Coach Moore yelled before she hit the next grounder to Addie at second and then Sophia at first.

When it was Zoe's turn again, the ball was hit to her left. Zoe took two quick steps and reached down for it, but it skipped off her glove and glanced over to Addie who picked it up and tossed it to first base.

"Argh!" she blurted out, kicking at some infield dirt. "I really blew that one."

"Reset button!" Ava called from third base, giving her a thumbs up.

Zoe nodded and returned the thumbs up gesture. As the other infielders caught the grounders, Zoe began to use her reset button. She drew in a deep breath through her nose before releasing it from her mouth. Then she grabbed some dirt, squeezed it, and tossed it back to the ground. She threw away her error! Finally, she tried positive self-talk.

"That play is over. You can't change it. You're a good fielder. Let's go! You got this!" She confidently said the words to herself under her breath.

Zoe walked back to her position; her eyes pinned on home plate. She noticed something different. Her heart no longer rapped against her ribs, her stomach relaxed, and her thoughts silenced. She was back in control.

The next ground ball was smoked and to her right. The softball skipped sharply off the dry dirt kicking up a dust cloud. Zoe took one quick step, backhanded the ball, set her feet, and fired it to Sophia at first.

"Now that's the way to do it!" yelled Mia from the outfield.

"Nice job! That was a big-time play," Addie cheered, smacking her hand in her mitt.

A rush of exhilaration billowed through her, and she bounced back to her position at shortstop and flashed them a grin. "Thanks!"

Zoe couldn't believe how effective the reset button was. The previous error was gone, and she was able to completely focus on the next play. She understood what Ava meant by playing softball one pitch at a time. It's the best way to play.

The rest of the practice went well. Zoe fielded ball after ball with just a few misplays. If she missed one, she did her reset and made the play on the next ball hit in her direction. As she walked off the field, she was brimming with confidence.

With the first game of the season fast approaching on Saturday, Zoe grinned. She and the Sting were ready for the season to begin.

3

The Cobras Slither into Southport

On Saturday, the rain pummelled Zoe's window, waking her. She climbed out of bed and stared out the window. The grey clouds mocked her.

Her stomach dropped as she realized they might not play today with the weather. Even after she stepped out of the shower and dressed, rain still rolled heavily down the window. It drummed on the rooftop and pooled on the ground below. She sighed, heading downstairs for breakfast.

"I hope the rain stops," Zoe said flatly as she slid into her seat at the kitchen table. She placed her head in her hands. "Typical luck on the opening day of the season."

Her dad shook his head as he buttered his toast. "Fear not, Zoe," he said, feigning an old English voice. "The phone says the rain will clear off by noon, and your game isn't until two."

"Oh, good!" Zoe said. She let out a sigh of relief and unclenched her jaw. "I'm ready to get started. We've had great practices, and I've become more confident. The new neighbor girl Ava taught me how to play softball one pitch at a time. She reminded me we can't change our mistakes. We can only focus on the next pitch because the next pitch is the most important in the game. Hanging around in the past will not help us win."

"Sounds like a wise new friend," her dad said, nodding along.

"Definitely. She taught me how to use my reset button if I make a mistake. I tried it, and it works! I'm really looking forward to a fun season."

"That's great. It'll be exciting to watch you play today. It's a new season and they are going to dedicate the new softball field. Go Sting!" he said as he gave Zoe a fist-bump and smiled.

***

Soon enough, the clouds drifted away and mist evaporated from the concrete as the sun beat down on Southport. Zoe cheered as the rays of sunshine reached through her window.

"We're going to play today!" she squealed.

She stepped into her black uniform pants and pulled the yellow softball jersey over her head. In black letters the word Sting was printed on the front and a logo of an intense looking hornet was on the left shoulder. Her eyes widened at the fierce logo in the mirror. She flexed her muscles to mimic the fierce look, but her toothy grin reflected back at her. She couldn't stop it from spreading across her face. Her parents waved goodbye to her as she raced out of the door. They would meet her at the game.

The sun warmed her back as she pedaled her bike to the ballpark. She could feel the energy in the air the moment she reached Archer Field. A large crowd was gathering, and music blared from the speakers. Balloons and streamers decorated the bleachers and danced in the light breeze. Today's game not only opens the season for the Sting, but it is a big day for the entire community. The game would be part of a ceremony celebrating the opening of the new softball field.

Zoe grinned and slowly scanned her surroundings, soaking up the festive environment. The sun was shining brightly, and she squinted, spotting Coach Moore in the dugout scratching out the line-up on her clipboard. Ava and several other players were in the outfield tossing the ball around. Mia was taking a few practice swings over by the backstop. The crowd was gathering in the bleachers and there was a rumble of chatter. The smell of popcorn popping sent salty, buttery scents across the field to her. Her heart pounded as she dumped her bag at the dugout, grabbed her mitt, and jogged to the outfield to join her team.

"It's softball season at last!" Addie blurted out. "We made it, girls."

"Ready to go?" Zoe asked as she joined Ava and Addie.

"Yes! I'm ready to go. Just remember, one pitch at a time. Use the reset button if you need to." Ava waggled her finger and smiled.

"You got it," Zoe responded with a confident nod.

***

Thirty minutes before game time, Coach Moore gathered everyone in the dugout.

"Okay girls! Are you ready? Let's go out there with energy and give it our all. The lineup is on the clipboard on the fence."

They turned their heads to see the Calabash Cobras looking back at them from across the field. Wearing brown pants, and white jerseys with gold lettering spelling Cobras across the front, they looked ready to play. The Cobras were a good team last year and added a new pitcher who was rumoured to be tough. They are sure to be one of the teams favored to win most games they play this year.

After the Cobras completed their infield practice, it was the Sting's turn to take infield. Zoe sprinted out to shortstop and scuffed up some dirt. While she waited for her first ground ball, she wiped her hand on her pant leg and pounded her mitt. During their warm-ups, Zoe and her teammates made every play. They were the home team, so they stayed on the field and anxiously awaited the first pitch.

Over the loudspeakers, the announcer bellowed out a welcome to all and played the national anthem.

Mayor Bob Archer took to the pitching circle to throw out the ceremonial first pitch. The lefthander fired a perfect strike to Hannah who was behind the plate. The packed house gave out a loud cheer and it seemed like all of Southport was ready for the softball season to begin. Both teams took their positions, and the umpire yelled, "Play ball!"

The Cobras' lead-off hitter was Victoria Brown. She was going to face the Sting's ace pitcher Emma Lopez. Emma was a tall, skinny kid who had an infectious smile and a strong desire to win. She was one of the area's best pitchers last year. Her fastball was feared by hitters. She also threw a wicked riser and changeup.

As Victoria stepped up to the plate and took her batting stance, Emma stood on the rubber and got the sign from Hannah King, the Sting's catcher. She wound up and fired the ball. The first pitch of the season was right down the middle. Victoria gritted her teeth and swung only to find air.

"Steeerike!" shouted the umpire as he stuck his right arm out in the air. The Sting's fans cheered.

Emma smiled, and Hannah couldn't help smiling too as she fired the ball back to the circle. After her next pitch was fouled off at home plate, Emma got Victoria to strike out on a high fastball.

"What a great way to start the season!" Ava called out to the Sting's pitcher as she caught the softball from Hannah and threw it around the infield.

Emma continued to throw strikes and quickly took care of the next two Cobras. One came on a slow grounder to first that Sophia easily fielded, and the third out came on a soft liner to Addie at second.

Now, it was the Sting's turn to bat, and the team sprinted toward the dugout. The Cobras were starting their toughest pitcher, Amelia Anderson. She had thrown a no-hitter last year. Zoe watched as Amelia fired her warm-up pitches. She could hear the catcher's mitt pop on each catch.

"She really throws hard! I don't think I have ever batted against anyone with that kind of fastball. I hope I can hit her," Zoe said to herself as she bit her bottom lip and fiddled with her batting glove. While she had new-found confidence in her fielding, she was not so confident with her hitting.

Addie LeMasters, the Sting's leadoff hitter, swung and missed Amelia's first two blazing fastballs. Addie was a tough hitter, and it was unusual for her to swing and completely miss two pitches in a row. She stepped out of the box and took a deep breath. Choking up on the bat, she stepped back in looking more determined.

"A little quicker, Addie!"

"You can get her!"

"Battle up there."

"You got this!"

The shouts rang from the stands and the Sting's dugout. Addie watched another fastball buzz over her head for ball one. She slapped the next pitch into right field for a hit. A huge grin was visible from behind the front bars of her batting helmet as she reached first base.

Next up was Grace Hill who was playing left field. After taking a fastball for a strike, she hit an easy fly to left field for the first out. Addie trotted back to first. The Sting's third hitter, Sophia Thomas, dug in and was ready to attack anything Amelia threw over the plate. She did just that as she slapped a hard grounder between first and second. Margaret DeConcini, the Cobras' second baseman, dove to her left and made a great stop. She scrambled to her feet and Sophia was thrown out at first on a very close play. Addie made a big turn at second before she wisely headed back to the bag. With two outs and a runner on second, the Sting's cleanup hitter Ava was next to the plate. The crowd and both benches began cheering loudly.

Ava walked with conviction to the plate. Even though she was playing with a new team and this was a big spot in the game, she looked confident, focused, and determined. Her crisp practice swings cut through the air. She looked down at Coach Moore in the third base coach's box before looking at her bat and then gazing out towards the pitcher.

"Hit your shot, Ava! Line-drive her! A base hit is a run!" the coach yelled as she clapped her hands enthusiastically.

The first pitch was in the dirt, but Ava swung anyway and missed it by a mile.

Zoe, who was watching closely, saw Ava look down at the coach again and then take a slow, deep breath. She looked at something on her bat, and then her eyes went to the pitcher. She seemed unfazed by missing the first pitch.

The next pitch was a fastball right down the middle. Ava swung and didn't miss this time. The softball met the bat with a loud ping and screamed towards the gap between the left and center fielders.

The Sting's fans sprung to their feet as the softball ricocheted off the fence. Addie ran as hard as she could, crossing home plate. By the time the Cobras' centerfielder tracked the softball down and fired it back into the infield, Ava was standing on third with a triple. Addie was surrounded as she made her way to the dugout and grinned ear to ear. Ava, all smiles, caught a glimpse of her parents and her brother, Luke, standing and clapping wildly in the stands behind the third base dugout. The Sting led 1-0!

Ava's eyes darted towards Zoe as she smacked her hands together.

"Great shot, Ava!" Zoe yelled loud enough to be heard over the crowd.

Amelia, the Cobras' pitcher, took off her glove and kicked some dirt. Her chest heaved as she took a deep sigh. She wasn't used to someone hitting a ball that hard off her. She was so flustered that she walked the next batter, Mia, on four straight pitches with none of them even close to the strike zone. The Sting now had two on with two outs, and it was Zoe's turn to bat.

As Zoe walked to the plate, her heart pounded. She looked around and saw the Sting's and Cobras' fans clapping and cheering. She heard the shouts of encouragement, some of which were for her and some of which were for the Cobras' pitcher.

As she got closer to home plate, her stomach churned. Her chest felt tight, and she felt and heard every heartbeat. She slowly looked down at Coach Moore.

"You can do it. Relax up there," said Coach Moore as she nodded and gave a soft fist pump. Zoe swallowed hard, trying to clear the lump in her throat. *How am I going to hit her?* she thought.

Zoe glanced over to the Cobras' dugout. She saw all the players up on their feet clapping and yelling. She could hear the Cobras' players saying things like, "You can get this girl, Amelia! Fire it past her! Strike her out! She can't hit!"

Zoe's legs quivered as she readied herself. Her hands were slick with sweat, and her mind raced as she rubbed one hand and then the next on her new, black pants trying to dry them.

It's like everyone is watching me. I am not sure I can hit her… I need to get a hit. What if I strikeout? The thoughts danced in her head.

Everything seemed to be going too fast. The umpire gave the signal to play ball. The Cobras' pitcher stepped on the rubber and looked at Zoe at home plate. Amelia's first pitch was a fastball, and Zoe swung.

Whoosh!

She missed it. The ball was by her before she even swung.

"Wow was that fast," she whispered, her eyes widening in surprise.

"A little quicker," shouted Coach Moore, clapping her hands again in encouragement.

Zoe stepped back into the box and hoped the next pitch would somehow be slower. It wasn't. But it was low, and Zoe didn't swing. Two more fastballs missed the strike zone making the count three balls and one strike.

All of those were by me before I knew it. Maybe she'll just walk me. I hope so. I'm not going to swing on the next pitch no matter what, Zoe thought. The next pitch was a fastball that zipped directly into the catcher's glove for strike two.

Wow, I didn't even see that one! I can't strike out. I just can't, Zoe thought, as panic set in. The count was now three and two.

Zoe stepped out of the box. Her heart thumped and her legs trembled a bit. It seemed like she could hear everyone in the stands and on the field even louder than before.

I wonder what the fans are thinking about me? Her mind raced. *Don't strike out! Whatever you do, don't strike out!*

"Let's go. Play ball!" the umpire said as he motioned for Zoe to get back into the batter's box so the game could continue.

Zoe cautiously stepped into the box, even though a small part of her didn't want to. She gazed out at the Cobras' pitcher who stared back in at her. Zoe noticed Amelia's scowl as the pitcher got her sign from the catcher.

Oh boy, Zoe thought.

The pitcher then hurled the softball towards home plate. It was a laser that flew right down the middle. Zoe froze.

"Steeerike three!" yelled the umpire turning and punching the air. The Cobras' fans and players went crazy as the team ran off the field. Zoe stood there in disbelief. Her mouth hung open, and her shoulders drooped. She quickly glanced at Ava down on third and felt even more disappointed.

"What just happened? It was right down the middle," she muttered. Her heart sank as she put her head down and slowly trudged to the bench.

"I should have swung at that one. I don't know why I didn't. I just froze. I can't believe it. That was terrible!" She kept murmuring about that last pitch as she grabbed her glove and made her way out to shortstop, still sulking. Zoe kicked some dirt, shaking her head. "Why didn't I swing? I can't believe it."

"Zoe! Zoe!" yelled Sophia, the Sting's first baseman. Zoe looked up just in time to see Sophia's infield practice ball rolling past her. She ran out into the outfield, picked it up, and tossed it across the diamond.

"Pay attention!" barked Sophia.

Zoe couldn't stop thinking about the strikeout. Gritting her teeth, she pounded her hand into her mitt. "You should have swung! You should have swung!" She said loud enough for the other Sting players to hear. It was all she could think about. She shook her head and kicked up some more dust.

Sophia tossed another warm-up grounder her way. Zoe took a few steps forward and tried to scoop it, but it skipped off her glove. The ball skidded away a few feet before Zoe finally grabbed it and flung it wildly toward first.

"Look out!" Sophia yelled, as Zoe's errant throw headed for the Cobras' dugout. Several players scrambled for safety as the softball slammed into the cement blocks of the dugout, narrowly missing them. Sophia tracked down the still moving ball and glared over at Zoe.

"C'mon, get in the game, Zoe!" Sophia yelled from across the field.

Ava, who was watching from third base, yelled, "Zoe, reset! Reset, Zoe! Get ready to win the next pitch."

Zoe looked over at her new friend and remembered Ava telling her softball is played one pitch at a time. The most important pitch is the next one. Your job is to get yourself ready to win the next pitch. Zoe took Ava's sound advice and put the Three Ts into action.

First, Zoe took some slow, deep breaths through her nose and down into her stomach, held the breath for a second, and blew it out through her mouth. She then picked up some dirt, squeezed it, and threw away the strikeout. It was like she was throwing the strikeout in the garbage.

"That strikeout is over! It's gone. I'm not going to think about it again. It's thrown away. Time to play great defense." She wiped her hand on her pantleg and smacked her mitt.

Zoe then did the very important last step. She told himself some positive things.

"You'll get her next time. You're a good hitter, Zoe. Now, it is time to be a quick-as-a-cat infielder."

Zoe snapped up the next practice ball and fired a strike to Sophia. No longer thinking about her strikeout, she felt a rush of confidence. The most important thing, however, was that she was focused on only one thing…the next pitch.

"Play ball!" said the umpire. As Emma stepped onto the rubber, Zoe looked toward the batter and felt sharp. She wasn't thinking about the strikeout. In fact, Zoe wasn't thinking anything. She was just ready to react!

It was a good thing too, as the Cobras' first hitter was Isabella Taylor. She was a big kid and the Cobras' cleanup hitter for a reason. Last year, she'd led her team in home runs. Isabella tightened up her batting glove and took a few hard practice swings before sending some dirt flying as she dug her back foot into the dirt. With teeth gritted, the batter seemed to dare Emma to throw her a strike. Emma got her sign from Hannah and went into her windup. She fired her best fastball towards the plate, and Isabella was waiting for it.

Crack!

A line-drive rocketed off her bat, right between shortstop and third. It looked like a sure hit. Zoe got a great jump on the ball, dove to her right, and speared it out of mid-air. She hit the ground hard, but the ball stuck in the webbing of her mitt.

"Out!" yelled the umpire, and the Sting's bench erupted in cheers. Isabella, bat still in hand, shook her head as she glared out at Zoe. Isabella couldn't believe it. She thought for sure she had a base hit.

"Nice job! Way to make a play," Emma said grinning as she got the ball back from Zoe.

From the dugout, Coach Moore yelled, "Great play, Zoe!"

Brushing some of the dirt off the front of her uniform, Zoe couldn't help but smile. The fans were still abuzz as a small cloud of dust drifted into the stands. Zoe glanced over at a grinning Ava.

"Way to reset! Way to reset!" Ava hollered over the crowd noise and gave a thumbs up. Zoe smiled back, pointed at Ava, and returned the thumbs up.

Zoe knew that Ava was one hundred percent right. If she had not reset, she would have still been moping about the strikeout and there's no way she would have been ready to make that great play. The three steps of the reset worked! She took some deep breaths, threw away the mistake, and told herself some positive things. She had been completely ready to win the next pitch.

Zoe bounced on the balls of her feet. "That's how you play softball—you reset and play one pitch at a time," she whispered to herself.

The game continued, and Emma got the next batter to hit a routine fly to Grace in left. But Hannah Hamilton, the Cobras' first baseman, smacked a double off the fence on a riser that didn't rise much. With two outs and a runner on second, Emma settled down and struck out the next hitter on four pitches. The Cobras would have scored a run had Zoe not reset and made that play on Isabella's line drive. The inning was over, with the Sting still leading 1-0.

Zoe and the rest of the Sting ran toward the dugout, eagerly awaiting their chance to bat. They wasted no time getting runners on base. Lily led off with a solid single to right that almost skipped past the Cobras' right fielder. Hannah King followed that up with a grounder that snuck through the hole between third and short. The Sting had something going. Two girls on with nobody out. Emma worked the count to two balls and no strikes before hitting a very high fly to center, which was caught by the Cobras' center fielder. One out. Two on.

Addie slapped a sharp ground ball right between first and second that chased Lily all the way home from second. Lily was all smiles as she pulled off her batting helmet and her now wet, red hair fell onto her shoulders. Addie hopped up and down on the first base bag. The Sting led 2-0.

The Cobras coach called timeout and jogged out to the circle where Amelia and the infielders had gathered. Whatever was said worked. The pitcher gave a confident nod, shifted her shoulders back, and slammed the ball into her mitt. She began throwing strikes and hitting the corners of the plate. Her fastball seemed get the zip back from earlier in the game. Her riser had even a sharper upward break to it. Grace struck out on three pitches. Sophia, the Sting's best hitter, also struck out after managing just one foul ball.

In the top of the third, the Cobras went quietly. Emma struck out the leadoff batter, and the second Cobras' hitter tapped a slow dribbler to first base that Sophia handled with ease. The third out of the inning came on a foul pop-up that catcher Hannah King corralled back by the backstop.

In the bottom of the inning, Amelia's warm-ups popped as they slammed into the catcher's glove. Ava was up first, and as she walked to the plate, Zoe noticed that even though Ava just saw her teammates strike out, she seemed unfazed. Ava did the same thing she did before each pitch. She looked at the coach, took a deep breath, looked at her bat, and then peered out at the pitcher. Ava saw that the first pitch was low and away for a ball. She swung at the next pitch and fouled it straight back. After she hit another foul ball, two more pitches missed the strike zone and made the count full at three and two.

The strong-willed Cobras' pitcher stood in the circle, staring in at her catcher. Zoe could tell Amelia was determined to get this first out of the inning. Ava kicked at the dirt in the batter's box and looked equally determined. It was strength against strength.

"You can win this!" Zoe hollered from the dugout.

Amelia went into her wind-up and let the pitch fly. Like a laser-guided missile, the ball whizzed through the air on its way to the catcher's target. It was right down the middle. Ava swung and…*whoosh*!

Nothing. Strike three!

The Cobras' fans clapped and shouted. Zoe watched as Ava calmly jogged back to the dugout and put her bat in the rack. She didn't slam her bat down. She didn't pout or mope. Instead, Zoe watched as her friend reset. Ava took a few deep breaths, grabbed a paper cup of water, drank it, crushed the cup, and forcefully threw it away. It was like that at bat was behind her.

Wow, Ava just used her reset. It was like it was automatic for her. Ava isn't being so hard on herself. She isn't pouting. She knows that she can't change that at bat but maybe she can get a hit the next time up. She is doing exactly what she told me to do—forget the mistake and just get ready for the next pitch, Zoe thought.

With Mia at the plate, Zoe's heart started beating faster as she put her batting helmet on and walked to the on-deck circle. She took some warm-up swings, but her stomach felt queasy again. She watched Amelia fire a first-pitch fastball past Mia.

"Wow, she's still throwing fast. She is throwing faster than the last time I was up. I hope she doesn't strike me out again," Zoe murmured as she rubbed the side of her face.

"Keep fighting, Mia. You can do it," shouted Coach Moore from the third base coach's box.

After missing a change-up, Mia quickly found herself down two strikes and no balls. Amelia was in the groove. The tall pitcher blazed another fastball that Mia missed with a late swing for strike three. A surprised Mia shook her head and walked back towards the Sting's dugout. The Cobras' ace pitcher was striking everyone out.

"Wow, she just struck out the last four batters. Mia never strikes out." Zoe gulped as she tightened her batting glove and tossed the extra warm-up bat aside. Her breaths were shallow, and a feeling of doom seemed to follow her to home plate. Zoe looked down at Coach Moore who, again, was clapping her hands in encouragement.

"Go get her, Zoe," coach said.

Zoe warily stepped into the batter's box and peered out at the Cobras' pitcher who looked even taller and meaner this time. Just like her last at bat, her heart pounded and her mind raced. A bead of sweat dripped down her cheek, and she scrubbed it off, trying to shake her nerves.

This pitcher throws so fast. Don't strike out like you did last time. She thought almost as if this reminder would somehow prevent such a thing from happening.

Amelia's first pitch blazed right by Zoe and smacked into the catcher's mitt with a loud pop for strike one. Zoe stood there, frozen to the ground.

Wow, I didn't even see that one. I bet she's going to strike me out again. Zoe thought as her shoulders slumped.

As she stood at home plate, it was like she could hear everything that was being said by the Cobras' fans in the stands.

"C'mon Amelia, blow it by her again!"

"Get her out!"

"She struck out last time!"

"This kid can't hit!"

Maybe they're right. I can't hit. Just don't strike out. Just don't strike out. Just don't strike out.

She squeezed the bat with an immovable grip. Her eyes darted from the stands to the pitching circle to the Cobras' infielders and back to pitcher. Each breath she took seemed to gather less air, and she tugged on the collar of her shirt.

The Cobras' pitcher quickly went into the windup, and Zoe could see the ball leave her hand, and then it was gone.

Whizz!

The ball shot by her before she even had a chance to start her swing. It was right down the middle.

"Steeerike two!" shouted the umpire.

Two pitches, two strikes, and she hadn't even taken the bat off her shoulder.

Zoe watched as the pitcher got the ball back from her catcher. She saw a slight smirk on the fearsome right-hander's face. Zoe could feel more sweat dripping off her forehead. From both inside and out, her mind was full of distracting chatter.

"I have to swing at the next strike. I can't just stand here and get called out again. Be ready and swing at the next strike," Zoe muttered.

"C'mon Zoe. You can do it!" Ava said from the dugout.

From the stands, Zoe heard her dad encouraging her. "Get your base hit, Zoe! Protect the plate!"

But Zoe also heard other things like, "Let's go, Amelia! You can get her! Strike her out again!"

Again. That word echoed in Zoe's head.

Don't strike out again! Swing if it's a strike. Don't just stand there like a statue! Zoe thought as she bit her bottom lip and wiped her mouth with the back of her hand.

Zoe carefully stepped back in and looked around the field. She gazed out at the tall, skinny righthander in the circle who seemed to be just standing out there, as if she was patiently waiting to strike Zoe out.

Amelia started her motion and let the ball fly. The softball nose-dived into the dirt about three feet in front of the plate, but Zoe swung! She missed it by a mile. She was so nervous; she hadn't even waited to see where the ball was going before she started her swing.

"Strike three," the umpire called as the Cobras' catcher scooped up the ball and tagged Zoe.

A thundering cheer went up from the Cobras' fans, and a long collective groan could be heard from those on the Sting's side.

Zoe smacked the top of her batting helmet with her hand and shook her head as she turned and made her way towards the bench. "I can't believe it. I just struck out again. What's going on?"

When she reached the dugout, Zoe took off her batting glove and jammed it into her helmet. "I am a terrible hitter," she said to Grace as she picked up her mitt. Grace gave her a quick pat on the back but didn't say anything. Zoe made her way to shortstop and put her head down completely deflated.

"I'll never be able to hit," she groaned.

Ava came over and slapped Zoe on the leg with her glove. "Hang in there. You'll get her next time. Remember, we need you on defense, so reset. Use those Three Ts."

Zoe nodded but couldn't even muster a slight smile. Even though she felt defeated, she knew Ava was right. She had to let this strikeout go and get herself ready to play each pitch on defense. This was a close game and pouting about her strikeouts wasn't going to help her team win.

She put the Three Ts to work. First, she took some deep breaths and then threw away the mistake by scooping up some dirt, squeezing it and tossing it down.

"Gone!" she said to herself. "That at bat is in the past, and I'm not going to give it another thought!"

For the last T, telling herself something positive, Zoe made sure to remind herself that she has a smooth swing and is a good hitter.

"All batters strike out sometimes. Next time up, I'll get her! Now, let's play a great shortstop. You got this!" she said.

In the top of the fourth, Emma continued to throw strikes. After giving up a lead-off bloop single, she struck out the next batter. With a runner on first, the dangerous Isabella Taylor was up. Emma was careful, too careful, and walked the big hitter on four pitches. The Cobras now had two on with only one out.

"C'mon, Emma. You can do it! Throw your game!" Addie called out slapping her glove and scratching the dirt with her cleats.

Emma settled down and struck out the next hitter, Casey Swift, and the inning ended when Hannah Hamilton hit an easy fly to right field. The Sting were still up 2-0.

The Cobras' ace breezed through that bottom of the fourth by getting Lily to ground out to second. Hannah struck out on a nasty rise ball, and Emma hit a soft line drive to the shortstop.

Emma started her fifth inning of work and still looked in fine form. Once the umpire said play ball, she went to work, getting the Cobras' catcher Makayla Whitaker to pop out to second. Louise Hernandez struck out on a 2-2 pitch for out number two. The Cobras' next hitter, Margaret DeConcini, hit a seeing-eye single between Ava at third and Zoe at shortstop. The Cobras' lead-off hitter Victoria Brown then smacked a hard grounder to second that Addie scooped up and fired to first for the last out of the inning.

In the bottom of the fifth, Addie grounded out to the pitcher and then Coach Moore sent Abigail Williams up to pinch hit for Grace. Abigail was a big, strong girl who hit the ball a long way...when she could hit it. Amelia Anderson who was still pitching for the Cobras, stared in towards home plate as Abigail stood at-the-ready. The Cobras' pitcher fired a fastball toward the inside of corner the plate. Abigail swung and the ball zoomed off her bat and soared a mile into the air toward left field.

In the dugout, the Sting's bench jumped to their feet and the crowd gasped. Could this be a home run? Would it clear the fence? The Cobras' speedy left fielder, Brooklyn Ward, sprinted back as the ball seemed to hang in the air forever. Brooklyn jumped as she got to the fence and the ball disappeared into her mitt. The Cobras' fans erupted in cheers.

"Nice swing!" Coach Moore said as Abigail jogged back into the dugout.

"Good job!" Ava said giving Abigail a fist bump. "You gave that one a ride. It was almost out of here!" Abigail flashed a quick smile and shook her head.

Sophia then flew out to deep center for the final out of the inning. As she headed to the dugout, she rolled her eyes and shook her head. She, too, thought she had a home run.

With the Sting still leading 2-0, Coach Moore called the team together and said, "This is it, one more inning. Let's go to work and finish this thing!"

The team sprinted out to their positions. If Emma could get these last three outs the Sting would win their first game of the season. They knew it wasn't going to be easy, though. The Cobras had their three best hitters coming up to bat this inning, including Isabella Taylor.

After finishing her warmups, Emma stood waiting for the first batter to dig in. Leading off the inning for the Cobras was Hailey Brooks. She was a scrappy hitter who rarely struck out. Emma quickly got ahead 0-2 on a couple of foul balls. She then tried to hit the corners on her next two pitches but missed. With the count 2-2, the next pitch was a solid one hopper, but it went right to Ava at third who made the play.

"Nice play, Ava!" Coach Moore yelled out from the dugout. Ava gave a quick nod without smiling, her eyes narrow and focused.

"One down, two to go," Addie shouted as she looked out to the outfield and waved her index finger in the air.

Next up was Claire Lewis, the Cobras' shortstop. She was also a very good hitter who always seemed to find a way to get on base. As if on cue, Emma's first pitch was lined right back up the middle for a base hit.

The tying run was now coming to home plate with one out.

All eyes shifted towards the Cobras' side of the field. It was Isabella Taylor's turn to bat. As the powerful hitter strode to the plate, her eyes were narrowed in determination, her shoulders back. The crowd fell silent in anticipation.

"Back up a few steps!" Coach Moore yelled and hurriedly motioned to the trio in the outfield who quickly backpedaled.

Zoe remembered that it was Isabella who hit that screaming line drive to her earlier in the game. She knew she had to be on her toes. Zoe, too, took a couple steps back. If Isabella ripped another one her way, she would be ready. As Isabella reached home plate, the fans of both teams began cheering the loudest they had cheered all game, but Zoe couldn't even hear them. Her eyes were focused on home plate. She was locked in.

The umpired signaled to play ball. The fans of both teams stood and yelled at a fever's pitch. Emma knew how good of a hitter Isabella was and had to be very careful with her pitches. In fact, she was too careful. Her first two throws were way out of the strike zone.

"Give her something to hit," Coach Moore shouted from the dugout, but she could barely be heard over the thunderous noise that filled Archer Field. "Trust your fielders!"

Emma stepped off the back of the rubber to reset. She took some deep breaths and rubbed up the softball. She then stepped on the pitching rubber, got the sign, and fixed her eyes on her catcher's target. Isabella stood at the plate with that same serious look on her face. She knew she was going to get her pitch, and she was more than ready.

Knowing she had to throw a strike, Emma put everything she had into the next pitch. It was a fastball, and it was on target. It was a strike right down the middle.

Crack!

The softball, which looked like a yellow blur, ricocheted off Isabella's bat in Zoe's direction. Zoe instinctively reached to her left and speared the one-hopper. Without a single thought, she set her feet and fired to Addie who caught it, jumped up to avoid the sliding runner, and made a perfect throw to first.

Sophia stretched out as far as she could at first base and snagged the throw.

"Out! Out!" the base umpire yelled punching the air twice with his arm.

That was the ballgame! A game-ending double play! The Sting and their fans were screaming and hollering. They had won 2-0!

Emma jumped in the air and then grabbed Ava by the shoulder and yelled, "We won! We did it! Can you believe it?"

The Sting bench swarmed the field, and there were high fives everywhere! Mia came running in from center field and smacked Zoe on her back with her closed mitt.

Wow! That's some kind of play you made! Two great plays in one game! Great job!" Ava said as she hugged Zoe.

Zoe smiled and said, "I would've never made that play if you hadn't taught me how to reset. You were right. No matter what has happened before in a game, it is this next pitch that matters the most. I was so ready for that ball."

"I could tell! Glad I could help!" Ava said.

Coach Moore joined them in their celebration on the field.

The Sting shook hands with the Cobras and headed back toward the dugout still bustling with excitement.

"Great game, girls! That's how to play softball! We have practice on Monday and another game on Wednesday night." Coach Moore beamed.

Zoe and Ava were giggling as they grabbed their gear and headed out of the dugout.

"Way to go! What a great way to start the season!" Ava turned her head to see her parents and Luke standing by the gate. Her mom and dad were all smiles. Luke was more interested in tossing pieces of popcorn into his mouth.

"Thanks!" Ava said as she and Zoe bounced their way toward them. "I can't believe we won that game. It was a tough one!"

"You made some super plays out there, Zoe," Mr. Davis said.

"Thanks!" Zoe replied still beaming.

"Dad, Zoe and some of the girls are going to watch the next game and want me to stay. Can I, please?"

Her father, still smiling, nodded yes, and said, "Here's some money for you girls if you want something to eat while you watch."

Ava playfully raised her eyebrows and turned to Zoe. "Oh yeah!"

"Thanks, and bye! I'll be home after the game!" Ava called out as both girls sprinted towards their Sting teammates who were gathered by the concession stand still buzzing about the exciting start to the season.

4

The Secret to Hitting

The next morning, Ava texted Zoe to see if she wanted to go to the batting cages. Zoe, still smarting from her bad at bats against the Wildcats, eagerly agreed to meet her. She figured she could use all the batting practice she could get. Zoe wanted to ask Ava if she had any ideas on how she could become a better hitter.

The morning sun was bouncing off the wet grass as the Ava knocked on Zoe's door.

"Hey there!" Zoe said as she opened the door, brushing her tussled hair to the side. "Let me get my stuff, and we'll get going."

As the girls started their short walk to the batting cages, they were still giddy about the team's victory.

"You made some great plays, Zoe. You were quite the shortstop out there."

"Thanks. Emma threw great, and you ripped the ball as usual," Zoe said, eyes wide. Then a serious look washed over her face.

"Can I ask you a question?"

"Sure." Ava sensed the concern in her new friend's voice. "What do you want to know?

"It's about hitting. When I bat, I get really nervous. It's like I hear everything, the fans, the other team, everything. My mind has a hundred thoughts going a million miles an hour. I am super distracted by what's going on inside my head, and the pitch goes by me before I know it." Zoe pursed her lips in frustration.

Ava nodded, and Zoe continued. "But I was watching you when you were batting, and you really seemed relaxed, focused, and confident. It was like nothing mattered except seeing the softball out of the pitcher's hand and ripping it. It was like you didn't hear the crowd or anything else going on. You were really locked in. How do you do that?" Zoe asked with a puzzled look on her face.

Ava listened intently and said, "Everything you just described is how I felt at the beginning of last year. I was always nervous and worried about striking out. I also remember talking to myself too much when I was in the batter's box. I would try to tell myself not to worry, to stay focused, and to not swing at a bad pitch. I would think about who was watching me bat and what they were thinking about me. I couldn't just focus on the pitch. The softball would come to home plate, and it was like I didn't even see it. It was so fast. I didn't get many hits at all, and I struck out a lot." Zoe gazed at the star player with a sense of disbelief.

The girls arrived at the batting cages. They had brought their bats, batting helmets, and a bag of balls. As they climbed inside the enclosed hitting area, Ava took her bat out of her bag and walked over to home plate.

Ava took a few slow practice swings. "At the very end of the season, I learned a skill that makes you a good hitter. I learned that when you're in the batter's box, right before the pitch is coming, you don't want to have any distractions at all. You want to stop thinking and just see the ball and hit the ball. I'll show you exactly how to do that."

"What do you mean by distractions?" Zoe said as she hung on every word.

"By that, I mean you don't want to be thinking about anything right before the pitch. You also don't want to talk to yourself either. It's called getting rid of the mental clutter. Great hitters have 'an empty mind.' This is what lets them see the softball out of the pitcher's hand and all the way to the plate. Nothing else matters! It is also called getting into the zone."

Zoe thought for a moment and said, "Yeah, it's sort of like when I'm really playing video games at my best. I can't hear anything else in the room, and I'm not really talking to myself or even thinking. I'm just really, really focused and reacting to the game."

"Exactly," Ava said. "Softball is all about reactions. You have to just react to the pitch. The only way to do that is to have complete focus on the softball coming out of her hand. The big secret is learning how to turn off all your thoughts right before the pitch."

"Wow, that would be great!" Zoe said eagerly. "Your lessons on how to calm down and reset really paid off. I bet this will too!"

Ava said, "Okay, the trick to getting relaxed and locked into the zone is using what's called a **pre-pitch routine**. A pre-pitch routine is something that a batter does before each pitch no matter what the situation is. There are four steps to a great pre-pitch routine. The cool part is that it is easy to learn, and with practice, you do it without even thinking about it. Do you want to try?"

"You bet!" Zoe grabbed her bat and eagerly joined Ava at home plate.

"**The first thing you want to do is to look down at the third-base coach** and see what the signs are. This is the only time you want to do any thinking."

Step 1. Look at Coach

Ava continued, "The next three steps are very important. Whenever you bat, you might be nervous, so **the second thing you do is take a slow deep breath**. It is the same kind of breath we talked about before with your reset. The breath goes in through your nose, into your stomach, and then blown out your mouth," Ava said. "It really slows everything down like your heart pounding and your racing thoughts. All the college players do it."

Step 2. Take a Deep Breath

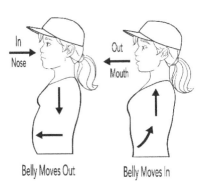

"I saw you doing that, too," Zoe said as her eyes widened.

"Yep, I do it every time," Ava said, grinning.

Ava stepped back to the edge of the netting and then walked up to the batter's box as if she was walking up to bat in a game. She looked down toward the imaginary coach, took a deep breath, and let it out. "Now you try it," she said.

Zoe pretended to look at her third-base coach and took a deep breath. "Can I take more than one if I'm still nervous?" she asked.

"Sure, that's a great idea. Sometimes, I'll take two or three if I need to. The main thing is to make sure you breathe in slowly and don't rush it."

After taking a few deep breaths, Zoe said, "Wow, that does help me feel relaxed! I could've really used it in the last game when I was facing Amelia. I was super nervous every time I was up. Once I have checked with the coach and take a deep breath or two, what is the next step?"

"**The third step is to turn off all thinking by looking at a small focal point on your bat.** It's probably the most important of all the steps. Remember when I said a batter doesn't want to be talking to herself or thinking anything? Using a focal point is like an on and off switch for a batter's thoughts. Many hitters use a small area on the bat to look at. It could be a scuff, a word, or a design on your bat. The important thing is that you really look at the fine details of focal point. You aren't thinking anything about the focal point just looking at it like nothing else matters in the whole world."

Step 3. Study Focal Point

Ava went on and said, "**Now, the last step is to move your eyes from the focal point right to the pitcher and stare at what is called the 'release point.'** The release point is a little window off to the side of the pitcher's leg where the pitcher lets go of the pitch. I sort of pretend it's like a video game and I'm looking for the softball coming out of that spot. You see the softball right away, and this makes it much easier to watch the ball all the way to home plate.

Step 4. Only Look at the Release Point

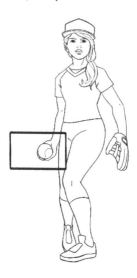

Don't look at the pitcher's face or anywhere else after you use the focal point. It would just distract you. Your eyes should go right from the focal point to the release point.

With the pre-pitch routine, I am not thinking. So, I am quicker to react to the pitch. If the pitch is outside of the strike zone, I let it go. If it is a strike, I rip it!"

Ava smiled and said, "It takes a little practice, but you'll get very good at using the focal point. Do you want to try it?"

"YES!" Zoe said. Ava grabbed a bucket of balls and headed to the pitching rubber while Zoe grabbed her new bat and stood by home plate.

"Now, Zoe, before each of my pitches, I want you to practice your pre-pitch routine. It may seem weird at first, but that's okay. It will get easier and easier the more you practice. The important thing is to do each step and try to get to the point where you're not thinking anything right before my pitch. Don't talk to yourself at all. The only thing that matters is the softball coming out of my hand."

With Ava ready to pitch, Zoe pretended that she was coming up to bat. She looked down at her coach, took a deep breath, and looked at her focal point which was a small scuff mark on her bat. Zoe studied it for a second like she had never seen it before. She zeroed in on the tiniest of details. She then looked out at the release point, which was just off Ava's pitching leg, down by her knee.

Ava let the pitch go and the next sound they heard was the solid crack of the bat smashing the softball! Zoe let out a little laugh and pumped her fist in the air as she watched the ball sail through the air. Ava flashed a toothy smile at the young hitter. Pitch after pitch,

Zoe took her time and practiced the four steps, and pitch after pitch, she connected.

Ava reached into the bucket for a couple more softballs. "Looking good. How does that feel?"

"It feels great! It's like I can really see the softball now. I'm not thinking anything or hearing anything. It's just me and the softball," Zoe said with a mile-wide grin. She felt a rush of newfound confidence.

"Okay, it's the last inning, there are two outs, and the winning run is on third. You're up. I'm going to try and strike you out," Ava said. Her face was serious, and Zoe could tell she was determined. Zoe went through her pre-pitch routine. She looked at the imaginary coach, took a deep breath, used her focal point, and peered straight out at the release point.

Ava's first pitch was a blazing fastball that was low and outside. Zoe saw it the whole way and let it go by.

"Good take!" Ava declared with a nod.

Again, Zoe took her time and did her routine before the next pitch. The next pitch was even faster than the first. It was a strike.

Crack!

The softball jumped off her bat and screamed past Ava's head as she ducked just in time.

"Wow, you almost got me with that one! Nice tip!" Ava said with a laugh.

For the next hour, the girls took turns playing an imaginary softball game, each trying to strike the other out. When they called it quits, they gathered up the softballs and met over by the water fountain.

"Wow, that was fun!" Zoe said. "The pre-pitch routine really helps. I can't wait to try it out at our next game."

"Well, you looked great there. You're looking like a whole new hitter. Pitchers, you better watch out, Zoe's coming after you!" Ava grinned and wiped the sweat off her forehead.

The girls packed their bat bags and headed home. As they reached Zoe's house, there was a new bounce in her step.

"Thanks again for teaching me the pre-pitch routine!" Zoe said. "I'll see you at the field."

"Sure thing. Go Sting!" Ava smiled and pointed her index finger to the sky.

5

The Wildcats Have Their Claws Out

The warm afternoon sun streamed into Zoe's room as she pulled on her team's uniform. Zoe knew it was going to be a perfect day for the Sting's next game. The Wilmington Wildcats were in town, and a bigger than usual crowd was expected at Archer Field. Even though it was only the second game of the season, it was an important one. Last year, the Wildcats and the Sting played each other four times with each team winning two games.

Zoe got to the field extra early as her teammates trickled into the ballpark.

"Ready to play today?" Zoe asked Mia as the girls dug into their bat bags for their gloves and a softball.

"I sure am! That was a great game we had against the Cobras, huh? I think we'll get these girls today," Mia said with a smug grin.

"It sure was a great game," Zoe said as she pounded her hand into her mitt. "Today's game is going to be another tough one. I heard the Wildcats are good again this year. When I was walking by the stands, I heard someone say that they beat the Rattlers 10-0 last game. Hey, who's pitching for us today?"

"I'm not sure, but I think it is going to be Sophia. Hopefully, she has her pitches working, especially her nasty change-up. That thing fools them every time," Mia said.

The girls went out into the outfield and started playing pitch and catch as the rest of the Sting players made their way into the park. Between throws, Zoe could see the concession stand was opening and noticed that the umpires stood and chatted to each other behind home plate. Coach Moore was in the dugout making the lineup and joking with the assistant coach.

The Wilmington players were huddled by their dugout, and booming chants from the group could be heard throughout the park. Each player wore a bright red uniform with WILDCATS emblazoned in gray across the front of their jersey. All the girls had matching bat bags and red spikes.

Mia and Zoe glanced at each other and gulped. The rest of the Sting also stopped warming up as they, too, gazed at the Wildcats who now sprinted out to right field, still hollering and whooping. The players got into lines of about four or five and started stretching. One of their players stood in front of the group and barked out which exercise was next. The Wildcats then paired up and made crisps throws to each other in silence.

Grace walked over to Mia, Ava, and Zoe and said, "Look at them. They're serious."

"And they're big too," Mia said. "Did you see that one girl? Number seven. She looks like she's in high school." Mia was referring to Natalie Wilson.

"She's good, too. Natalie pitches and plays first base for them and can really hit. I think she was the leading home run hitter in the league last year," Grace said.

"I hope she isn't pitching today," Zoe muttered, still staring out at the fearsome pitcher. A swarm of butterflies took flight in her stomach.

Unfortunately, Zoe didn't get her wish. The Wildcats finished throwing to each other in the outfield and started running towards the dugout for infield warm-ups. Everyone ran to the dugout except for Natalie and her catcher who stayed in the outfield to warm up. She was, indeed, going to be the starting pitcher.

The Wildcats took their infield practice with high energy and precision. They were a well-oiled machine. Meanwhile, Coach Moore called all the Sting into the dugout, her lips set in a tight line. "This is a very good team and a very good pitcher we're playing today. Remember, you girls are good too. Now, let's get out there and give it everything we've got!"

Coach then read off the starting lineup. Sophia, the starting pitcher for the Sting, and her catcher, Hannah, trotted down to the Sting's bullpen to loosen up. The rest of the team took their positions in the field. Coach Moore started hitting ground balls to the infielders and fly balls to the outfielders. Zoe and the rest of the Sting looked sharp and ready to play.

After infield warm-ups, the umpires met with the coaches from both teams at home plate to go over the ground rules. All shook hands, and Coach Moore shouted, "Let's go! Take the field! C'mon Sophia, go get them!" The Sting scrambled out of the dugout, and Sophia jogged out to the pitching circle.

During her warm-up throws, the lefthander's fastball had some extra zip on it, but her riser and changeups just weren't finding the plate. Her riser was way too high, and her changeup was bouncing in the dirt. After each failed throw, Sophia shook her head and swung her arm without the ball, trying to get a feel for her pitches.

"She's really struggling," Addie said to Emma who was playing first base today. "That's not like her." Emma raised her eyebrows and nodded in agreement.

"Play ball!" the umpire shouted, and the Wildcats' lead-off hitter, Olivia Wellington, tossed down the extra bat she was swinging on-deck and marched to home plate with her chin high, chest puffed out. Olivia was a strong, athletic girl who was a very good hitter. She stepped to the plate, her jaw clenched and her eyes glinting with startling fierceness. With her foot, she dug a hole near the back white line of the batter's box.

Olivia smacked her black bat on the outside corner of the plate and focused her stare out at Sophia. The pitcher got her sign from Hannah. It was going to be a rise ball. Sophia went into her windup and let the first pitch of the game go.

Crack!

The Wildcats' hitter swung and clobbered the ball. The softball jumped off her bat like it was shot out of a cannon and screamed skyward. It was high and deep, way deep towards center field. Mia sprinted to the fence and leapt backwards, but the softball disappeared from everyone's view. The Wilmington players whooped and hollered as they poured out of the dugout to greet Olivia at home…one pitch, one run.

Zoe glanced over at Ava, and mouthed the words, "Wow, that was a shot!"

Ava bit her lip and nodded as the umpire tossed Sophia a new softball.

"What a way to start the game," a shocked Sophia muttered as she rolled her shoulders back and shook her head.

Sophia didn't have too much luck with the next two hitters, and they both reached base with singles.

The Wildcats' second baseman, Rhannon Adams, slapped a blooper to right, and their shortstop, Rachel Lee, smacked a hard ground ball up the middle and into center field.

It was now time for Wildcats' cleanup hitter, Natalie Wilson, to bat. Sophia was surely in a jam, and it wasn't going to be easy to get out of this inning. Natalie towered over Hannah and could look eye-to-eye with the home plate umpire. She took a few aggressive practice swings and smacked the bottom of her cleats with the bat. She glared as she stepped into the batter's box as if she owned that small piece of property. Sophia rubbed the side of her face, letting out a shaky breath as she glanced into the Sting's dugout.

"You're alright. Go after her," Coach Moore yelled out to her struggling pitcher.

Sophia stepped on the pitching rubber and got her sign from Hannah. Her first pitch was a rise ball that sailed high and almost went to the backstop had Hannah not made a great snag. The second pitch wasn't much better. It was a change that landed way in front of the plate, and Hannah dove out and blocked it, keeping both runners at their bases. Sophia's third pitch, a fastball, was way inside and missed the strike zone too, so the count reached three balls and no strikes. Sophia's shoulders drooped and she stared at the ground in front of her. Hannah called time out and traipsed out to Sophia, brows knitted together. The Sting infielders joined her in the circle.

"What do we throw on 3-0 to the best hitter in the league?" Sophia whispered, squinting at her catcher.

"Well, you need to throw a strike. We don't want to walk her. Give her your best fastball, but keep it low," Hannah offered.

"Got it," said Sophia as she shook her head, lips tight together. Hannah jogged away and settled in behind home plate. The umpire pointed towards the pitcher and signaled for the game to continue. Zoe watched as Sophia took off her hat, wiped some sweat from her forehead, and stepped back on the pitching rubber.

From the third-base coach's box, the Wildcats' Coach Smith said, "She has to throw you a strike, Natalie. Be aggressive. If it's there, hit it!"

The hoots and hollers from the Wildcats' faithful fans in the stands grew louder and louder. The

Wildcats' players spilled out of the dugout clapping and chanting like chimpanzees ruling the jungle.

Natalie snapped the bat in front of her twice, practicing her swing, then arched her back and dug back into the batter's box. She knew she was going to get a good pitch to hit. The tall batter eased her bat back and forth as she awaited Sophia's next offering.

The Sting's pitcher reached inside her glove and grabbed the softball with her fastball grip and let the pitch fly. It was low, just like Hannah wanted. It was also in the strike zone. Natalie was ready and took a huge swing and connected. The softball shot off her bat. It was a line drive right at Zoe.

Smack!

The shortstop caught it without even flinching. The ball was hit so hard that the runner who had taken a big lead off second just froze. She had no chance to get back before Zoe tagged her. Double-play! Two down!

Now it was the Sting's bench, and their fans' turn to erupt in cheers.

"Way to go, Zoe!"

"Nice play!"

"Alright Sting!"

"Two outs!"

"Nice play, Zoe! Now, let's get this last out, Sophia," Ava hollered above the crowd noise. She smacked the palm of her glove as she ran back to her position at third base.

Sophia breathed a big a sigh of relief but knew she still had to wiggle her way out of the inning. The next hitter for the Wildcats was their right fielder, Leah Clark. In the batter's box, Leah wore a smug grin, loosening her shoulders as she tapped her cleats with her bat and took some warm-up swings. Sophia sent her first pitch towards the plate. Leah let it go by. It was a strike. She also let the next three pitches go by with two of them being outside the strike zone and a third catching the inside corner. The count was now 2-2. Sophia stared in for the sign. Hannah wanted a riser. Sophia nodded in agreement and tossed her next pitch towards home plate. The pitch was headed right down the middle of the plate before rising sharply. Leah swung—strike three!

"Great time for you to find your rise ball!" Zoe slapped Sophia on the back as they sprinted to the dugout.

Down 1-0, it was the Sting's turn to bat in the bottom of the first. From the dugout, all eyes were fixated on the Wildcats' pitcher, Natalie Wilson. She towered in the circle, and her pitching motion was smooth as silk. Her fastball was like lighting. One pitch after another went *pop*, *pop*, *pop* as each hit the catcher's mitt.

From the dugout, Zoe carefully studied each pitch. She noticed that after one of the warm-ups, the catcher even took her hand out of her mitt and shook it to try and get the sting to go away.

"Wow, she has a blazing fastball. Natalie is the fastest pitcher I've ever seen," Zoe said to Ava.

"She is fast, but you can hit. Just remember the pre-pitch routine and focus on one pitch at a time. Remember, all you have to do as a hitter is win one pitch. Just one pitch. That's all," Ava declared confidently.

Addie LeMasters was first up for the Sting. The skinny second baseman wore number seven on the back of her jersey. She had a knack for always making contact no matter who was pitching. In fact, Addie only struck out one time all season last year. As she stepped into the batter's box, the crowd and both dugouts came to life. The first pitch to Addie was a fastball that seemed to be by her before she even knew it. She didn't swing. Strike one. Addie backed out of the box; her eyes wide.

"You got this, Addie! You're a good hitter!" one of the Sting players yelled from the dugout.

Natalie got the sign from her catcher and fired the next pitch at the same speed. It also found the target. Again, Addie just stood there and watched it zip by. Strike two.

The Wildcats' catcher yelled, "Great pitch," and fired the ball back to her pitcher. Natalie quickly went into the windup and hurled the softball plate ward.

Again, it was a blur.

"Steeerike three!" the umpire shouted as Addie stood motionless at the plate. In a state of shock, Addie's mouth hung open for a second before she plodded her way back towards the bench. As she reached the dugout, there were words of encouragement from her fellow teammates.

"Tough one."

"You'll get her next time, Addie."

"You're okay."

Addie shook her head, still a bit stunned by how quickly her at bat was over. She plopped down at the far end of the bench to see what Grace could do against the Wildcats' ace. After all, Grace was also one of the team's better hitters. Unfortunately, it happened again. Another strikeout. This time it was four pitches without Grace making any contact. The same fate awaited Sophia. Three strikes, all of them swings and misses. Like the hitters before her, Sophia couldn't connect with any of the pitches. The inning was over.

"Wow, three strikeouts and not even one foul ball was hit," Zoe said softly.

The Sting's dugout was unusually quiet as the girls grabbed their mitts and headed out to the field. It was like all the wind had been knocked out of their sails. They'd never seen a pitcher this good.

Sophia took her warm-up tosses and was set to face the next three Wildcats' hitters. The first batter was Michelle Benson, the Wildcats' third baseman. She fouled off the first two pitches before hitting a routine fly to center that Mia caught with ease. Sophia didn't have much trouble with the next two Wildcats either, as she got Samantha Weaver to ground out to first and right fielder Katie Cole grounded out to

Addie at second base. It looked like Sophia had settled down after that rough first inning.

Due up for the Sting in the bottom of the second were Ava, Mia, and then Zoe. The umpire signaled batter up, and Ava walked to the plate. She looked down at Coach Moore before taking a deep breath and looking at a small spot on her bat. Her eyes then flicked towards the release point.

"She is doing her pre-pitch routine," Zoe said quietly to herself as she closely watched Ava's actions.

Natalie's first pitched sped towards the plate. Ava swung and missed. Like the other Sting, she was too late on the pitch. As the catcher tossed the ball back to the pitcher, Ava calmly did her pre-pitch routine. She glanced at the coach, took her deep breath, looked at the focal point on her bat, and then stared out at the pitcher's release point. Natalie went into her windup and threw her first change-up of the game. It was a good one, and Ava came up empty on an early swing. The count was no balls and two strikes, a hitter's least favorite count.

Zoe noticed something. Even though Ava had swung and missed on the first two pitches, she stuck with the same pre-pitch routine.

"It only takes one! Go back to work!" Her third-base coach called out.

Natalie's next pitch was a fastball that sailed high, and Ava let it go by. After missing outside with a pitch, the next pitch was a fastball that found the strike zone. Ava swung and made solid contact, but it was a line drive right at the left fielder who made the catch.

"Well, at least someone finally hit the ball," Addie said with an eye roll.

The Sting's next hitter, Mia, was unable to do the same. She swung too late on two fastballs and struck out by flailing at a change-up in the dirt. Natalie had struck out four of the first five Sting hitters. Two down, and it was Zoe's turn to bat.

As she was walking to the plate, Zoe chewed her lips and her palms sweated. Her heart thumped in her chest; thoughts swirled wildly in her head. Just before she reached the batter's box, she heard something from the Sting's dugout.

"You know what to do, Zoe! You know what to do!" It was Ava.

Zoe nodded, drawing in a deep breath. She was going to use the pre-pitch routine Ava taught her. She looked down to the coach at third, took another deep breath and then looked at that small spot on her bat, her focal point to turn her thinking off. Her mind was silenced, and she was ready for the pitch. Zoe focused out at the release point and nothing else. She was going to see the softball all the way from the pitcher's hand to home plate.

Natalie took her windup and threw her first pitch. It was a fastball in the strike zone. Zoe swung. The bat rattled in her grip as it connected with the ball. The ball soared skyward towards the right field fence.

Is it over her head? Will it be a homer? Zoe wondered, filled with instant excitement.

She sprinted towards first and glanced up just in time to see the Wildcats' right fielder make a great leaping catch at the fence. Although it was the third out of the inning, Zoe felt a rush of confidence. She had just ripped a shot off a Natalie Wilson fastball!

Zoe took off her batting helmet and handed it to the first base coach who was heading back to the dugout. She jogged towards her position at shortstop still smiling at her near home run.

Ava handed her glove to her and said, "Way to put the bat on the ball. I saw your routine! I told you it works!"

"Thanks!" Zoe couldn't contain her smile as she slid her hand into her mitt and gave it a quick smack.

As Mia passed by on her way to center field, she said, "Nice swing. I thought that one was out of here!" Zoe grinned and nodded, all smiles.

It was now the top of the third with the Wildcats still leading 1-0. Sophia had settled into a good groove. She struck out the first two Wildcats, and the third out was an easy grounder to first base. In the bottom half of the third inning, the Sting also went just as quickly with Lily grounding out to the pitcher and both Hannah and Emma striking out.

In the top of the fourth inning, Sophia had to face the heart of the Wildcats' order with hitters three, four and five. Rachel Lee, Natalie Wilson, and Leah Clark were due up. All were good hitters. Sophia took her warm-up pitches. Her fastball still popped the mitt, but she started having trouble again with her rise ball.

"Play ball," the umpire said, and the first batter came to the plate.

Sophia's first pitch was a fastball for a strike. The second pitch was the same. She then threw a change-up that bounced in the dirt, but Rachel didn't bite. With the count 1-2, the Wilmington shortstop hit a ground ball between first and second. Addie made a diving stop, scrambled to her feet, and threw to first.

"Out," shouted the first base umpire. It was a close play. In fact, it was so close that the Wildcats' fans could be heard grumbling loudly along the first-base bleachers. Rachel scowled as she traipsed back to the dugout. One out.

Natalie Wilson, the cleanup hitter, was up next.

"This girl can hit. Back up a few," Mia called out to her fellow outfielders.

In her first at bat, she rocketed a line drive that Zoe at shortstop caught and turned into a double play. With Natalie in the box, staring out at Sophia, the pitcher got her sign from Hannah. Hannah wanted a riser. The Sting's pitcher nodded in agreement. Natalie smashed her best fastball the last time she was up, so she would try something different. Sophia went into her windup and let go of the pitch. It was a pitch that she wished she could've had back. It was a rise ball that didn't rise at all.

Natalie took a huge swing and blasted the ball towards left field. The yellow softball disappeared into the sky, easily clearing the fence. Like ants pouring out of an anthill, the Wilmington players streamed from their dugout to greet the tall slugger. Natalie grinned in triumph as her teammates barreled towards her, reaching high to slap her batting helmet as she crossed home plate.

The Wildcats now led 2-0. Watching the celebration continue, Sophia got a new softball from the umpire and smacked her leg with her glove. She kept looking over at the still jubilant Wildcats and their fans. Everyone could tell Sophia regretted throwing that pitch. Coach Moore called time out and walked out to talk with Sophia. The Sting's infielders also gathered around their coach and pitcher.

"Okay, girls that was one swing. We're still in this game. We'll score some runs. Let's play one pitch at a time and get out of this inning. You can do it, Sophia. Just keep throwing your strikes. Let's go!"

"You got this!" Zoe said with a confident nod.

The home plate umpire walked toward the group, and the meeting broke up just before he got there. The Sting hustled back to their positions and Sophia stood in the circle, her forehead still tense.

Leah Clark, the right fielder, dug in at the plate. Sophia started Leah off with a fastball that backed her away from the plate. The next pitch was a changeup, and Leah hit a high chopper to short that Zoe played perfectly and fired to first for the second out of the inning.

"Alright! That's the way to play!" Sophia shouted and smacked her glove against her leg.

Michelle Benson, the next hitter, could only manage a soft fly to left field that Grace grabbed for the last out of the inning.

In the bottom of the fourth inning, trailing 2-0, the top of the Sting's order was up. Natalie was throwing a no-hitter and had recorded six strikeouts already. The Sting knew they needed to get something going, and they did just that.

Addie started the inning by coaxing a walk. After fouling off three straight 3-2 pitches, she let a low outside fastball go by for ball four. With a runner on first, Grace found herself quickly down 0-2. On the next pitch, she swung at a low changeup and barely hit it. It was a slow roller that the charging second baseman couldn't get before the ball stopped. It was a lucky infield hit. Down by two, the Sting had the tying runs on base with nobody out.

The Wildcats' coach called time-out and slowly walked out to talk to her tall righthander and the teams' infielders. The Sting's fans were buzzing with excitement on the third base side while the Wildcats' fans were somewhat more subdued. After the meeting broke up and the players returned to their positions, the umpire pointed towards the pitcher and gave the signal to play ball.

"C'mon, Sophia! Bring them in!" Zoe yelled as she clapped her hands in the dugout.

Sophia marched up to the plate. Like the two hitters before her this inning, she also had a good at bat. She kept fouling off pitches before she smoked a hard liner, but it was right at the Wildcats' third baseman for the first out. Both Sting's runners scampered back to their bases so there was no double-play on the line drive.

Now, it was Ava's turn to bat. Sensing a big moment in the game, both benches and everyone watching in the stands got louder and louder.

"Hit your shot! Right hitter, right time!" shouted Coach Moore before looking out at second base at Addie. "Get a good jump out there, Addie. You're scoring on a hit!" the coach called out, raising her voice so she could be heard over the very loud crowd. Addie nodded.

By now, all the Sting players were standing at the edge of the dugout clapping and cheering. "This is our chance," Zoe said to Hannah who was standing next to her.

"She's going to do it! Ava is going to get a hit," Hannah said assuredly.

Ava took some crisp warm up swings, did her pre-pitch routine, and stepped in the box. The first pitch was high for ball one. Natalie missed with her second pitch also, this time outside. The third pitch was a fastball that sailed high. The count was suddenly three balls and no strikes. It was a hitter's count for sure. In the stands, the Sting's fans were hysterical with excitement. The team had two on with a 3-0 count on their best hitter.

"She has to come to you, Ava. Rip it!" Grace yelled loud enough to be heard over the boisterous crowd.

Natalie stood in the circle her eyebrows scrunched. This was the first jam she'd been in all game. She didn't dare walk Ava to load the bases, but she also had to be careful since she knew she was facing a great hitter. She tugged on the collar of her shirt and then stepped on the pitching rubber, gazed in towards her catcher, and let the pitch fly. It was a fastball. The next sound everyone at Archer Field heard was the crack of the softball meeting the bat. It was a clean base hit between left and center field.

"Go, go, go!" Coach Moore yelled to Addie as she windmilled her arm through the air. "Get in there!"

Addie scored easily as the ball came into the shortstop. Grace held on at second and Ava rounded first before heading back to the first-base bag. The score was now 2-1, with the tying run on second and the go ahead run on first. One out.

While Mia walked towards home plate, Zoe moved into the on-deck circle, tightening her batting glove. She took a few practice swings and noticed her quickened pulse and knotted stomach.

"Take some deep breaths and remember to do your pre-pitch routine. It's just you and the softball. Nothing else matters. See it and hit it," she said softly to herself as she swung a bat.

After throwing a fastball for a strike, Natalie's next pitch was a fastball. It was inside, too far inside, and hit Mia on the elbow.

"Take your base," called the umpire. Mia winced, shook her arm a bit, and jogged to first. The bases were now loaded for Zoe. The home crowd erupted in cheers.

Walking to the plate Zoe thought about her last at bat against Natalie. *I smashed one to right field off her last time. I can do it again.* Shoulders back and chin up, determination washed across her face.

Zoe looked down at the third base coach, took her deep breath, looked at the focal point on her bat, and zeroed in on Natalie's release point. The roar of the crowd was merely a dull hum in Zoe's ears. She was focused. She wasn't thinking about what could happen. She wasn't trying to talk to herself or coach herself on swinging or not swinging, and she wasn't even worrying about what anyone was saying or thinking about her. It was just complete concentration on the pitcher's release point.

Natalie took some extra time and walked around the circle, rubbing up the softball. She then stepped on the rubber, got her sign, and hurled a fastball towards her catcher's open mitt. The spinning softball was coming right down the middle. Zoe swung and felt a firm jolt. The softball jumped off her bat. It was a line drive right back at Natalie. As the speeding ball shot straight at her head, the tall pitcher ducked and instinctively stuck up her glove.

Thwack!

The ball somehow found Natalie's mitt as she tumbled awkwardly to the ground. Zoe had barely taken a step toward first and was still holding her bat when the umpire yelled, "Out!"

"Great swing! Way to put the bat on it!" the third-base coach shouted. Zoe gave a quick shake of her head and smiled softly as she trotted back to the dugout. She caught a glimpse of her dad who was smiling and gave a small pump of his fist.

"Nice rip up there! You almost took her head off with that liner!" Hannah said giving Zoe a high five.

"Thanks, it felt good coming off the bat. I just can't believe she caught it," Zoe said as she rolled her eyes and stood in the dugout.

Lily stepped to the plate. After getting her sign from her catcher Natalie sent the next pitch to the plate. It was a great change-up that started out in the strike zone but dropped towards the dirt. Lily was fooled on the pitch and hit a soft groundball to the first baseman who scooped it up for the third out of the inning. The rally was over, but the Sting did get one run to cut the lead in half.

In the top of the fifth, Sophia continued to throw well. Wilmington went down in order. Samantha Weaver grounded out to the pitcher. Katie Cole was called out on a nasty fastball that caught the inside corner. The ninth hitter in the order, Mila Smith, struck out again for the second time in the game to end the inning.

It was the bottom of the fifth, and the Sting needed another rally. Abigail, pinch hitting for Hannah, led off the inning by taking three huge swings. The first two swings connected but were long foul balls down the right-field line, but she came up empty on her third swing and struck out. Emma was next and hit the first pitch on a line to the second baseman for the second out. Addie followed with a single. Grace stepped in and would work the count full, three balls and two strikes, before ripping a wicked one hopper to short. The Wildcats' shortstop fielded it cleanly and made a quick flip to second to end the inning. Grace grimaced and put both hands on her helmet as she trotted back to the dugout.

"Let's hold them. We still have one more at bat!" the coach said to the team as they grabbed their gloves and sprinted out to the field. Even though they were disappointed they didn't score, the Sting didn't quit. The first batter to face Sophia in the sixth was Olivia Wellington. She was the Wildcats' lead-off hitter who opened the game with a homer. Sophia knew she had to be careful. This needed to stay a one-run game.

Her first pitch to Olivia was a fastball that was on the outside corner, right where Sophia wanted to throw it. The slugger swung and hit a long fly to right field that sent Lily back a few steps before she caught it for the first out. Rhannon Adams, the second baseman, was up next and, just like her first time up, she stuck her bat out and hit a single into the outfield. That was the only hit the Wildcats could muster in the inning. Sophia struck the next hitter out on a good riser and then got the dangerous Natalie Wilson to fly out to Mia who made a nice running catch in deep center field. The score was still 2-1.

The bottom of the sixth was the Sting's last chance, and it would be Sophia, Ava, and Mia to start the inning. It was now or never!

"Play ball!" the umpire shouted. Both dugouts yelled encouragement to their teammates and the fans started getting louder and louder. Sophia stood in the box and knew she needed to somehow get on base. The first pitch was a fastball that almost hit her, but the next two pitches were called strikes. Sophia swung on the next pitch and hit a hard grounder to second. The second baseman bobbled the ball but quickly grabbed it and fired an accurate throw to first, beating the hustling Sophia by a half-step. One down.

Ava was up next and tossed the extra warm-up bat down in the on-deck circle and slowly walked towards home plate. Once again, the crowd roared and stamped their feet. Ava looked down to the coach, took her deep breath, and briefly stared at that small spot on her bat before looking towards the pitcher. Zoe knew she wasn't looking at the pitcher but at the release point. Her eyes were going to zero in on the softball coming out of the pitcher's hand. The Sting needed a hit.

Zoe nodded her head in Addie's direction. "She looks confident and relaxed like she always does."

Addie shook her head in agreement. "C'mon Ava, you can do it!"

With Ava ready at the plate, Natalie stared at her catcher for the sign. She gave a quick nod and went into her windup. The pitch was just as fast as any of the ones she had thrown in the innings before. Ava swung and made solid contact. The ball sped off her bat and ricocheted foul down the left field line before bouncing hard off the side fencing.

"You're right on her, Ava!" Coach Moore yelled from the third-base coach's box. "Get something started for us."

Ava went through her pre-pitch routine exactly as she had before. Her eyes then went right out to the release point. Natalie's next pitch was another heater that was high, and Ava let it go by for ball one. Again, Zoe watched as Ava did the same pre-pitch routine.

"She does it every time, just like she told me," Zoe whispered to herself.

Just as that thought came out of Zoe's mouth, Natalie let fly another fastball. This one was down the middle about knee high. Ava swung and connected. It was a low line drive to center field that bounced in front of the fielder for a clean base hit. Zoe and her teammates perked up at the sight of Ava running down to first and making the turn before returning to the first base bag. The Sting had the tying runner on base.

Mia Jennings was the next to bat. The Wildcats' pitcher still seemed confident and in control as she tossed her first pitch towards the plate. It was too low. Ball one. After throwing two fastballs for strikes and missing with another fastball, the count was two balls and two strikes on Mia. Ava clapped her hands at first base. Natalie went into her windup and fired one of her best fastballs. Mia swung and ripped a high fly ball to deep center which was caught back by the fence. Ava alertly tagged up and scrambled into second base. Two outs. The Sting were down to their last out. It was up to Zoe to keep the game going.

As she walked to the plate, Zoe noticed she was getting nervous. This was a big at bat for sure. It was the last chance for the Sting. Zoe's heart pounded, and her mind started going a million miles an hour. Zoe looked out at Ava on second base and Ava motioned for her to take a deep breath and do her pre-pitch routine.

When she reached home plate, Zoe did just that. She looked down at her coach, then she took not one, but two slow deep breaths. Zoe took a second to stare at the small spot on the bat. This was her "thinking off switch." Her eyes went out towards the pitcher's release point. She wasn't as nervous, and most importantly, she wasn't thinking anything. She was ready. All that mattered was the softball coming at her from Natalie's hand. Zoe was going to focus on the ball and nothing else.

Natalie started her motion and fired the first pitch to Zoe. The speeding softball was on target. Zoe swung and the bat vibrated. As the softball jumped off her bat, she knew it was a hit and instantly heard loud screams of "Go, go, go!"

Zoe dashed towards first and craned her neck up to see the softball landing in the gap in between the center fielder and the right fielder. No one was going to get it until the softball bounced up against the fence. Zoe put her head down and ran as fast as she could. The first base coach waved for her to go to second. As she was getting to the bag, she saw the Wildcats' shortstop jump up to catch the throw in from the right fielder. Zoe slid hard into second base and felt her left foot slam into the bag right before the shortstop's glove slapped her on the back.

"Safe!" the umpire shouted as a dust cloud surrounded the players.

During the play, Ava hustled home from second base. The Sting tied the game 2-2! Zoe stood on second base with a huge smile on her face. She clapped her hands wildly and then brushed some dirt off her uniform, too excited to stand still. The Sting's fans were cheering at a fevered pitch, and Zoe saw her parents clapping and celebrating! She looked over at Coach Moore who hollered out to second, "Nice hit! Way to go, Zoe!"

The Sting's bench greeted Ava after she crossed home plate with the tying run and then turned their attention to Zoe out at second base.

"Good job, Zoe!"

"Great rip."

"You did it girl!"

Zoe continued to clap her hands and bounce up and down on second base.

The crowd hummed as Lily came to bat. Lily blazed with determination after seeing Zoe's double. Meanwhile, Natalie Wilson let out a grunt, scuffing her cleats in the dirt, knowing she gave up the big hit. The Wildcats' pitcher pounded her mitt and stomped around in the circle. She shook her head in disgust and looked up at the sky before she was ready to pitch.

Natalie's first pitch was right down the middle, and Lily swung and ripped a foul straight back for strike one.

"A base hit here wins the game," someone screamed from the stands.

Zoe's body tensed like a lion ready to pounce as she prepared to run on anything. She was going to score on any base hit.

The first pitch was also a fastball that Lily drilled into the Sting's dugout. With the count 0-1, Lily fouled two more pitches off. With each foul ball, Natalie's frown deepened, and a red flush crept up her cheeks. The Wildcats' ace was looking for a strikeout, and Lily was hitting her best fastballs. Natalie decided to reach back and throw the next fastball with all her might. She flung the softball towards home plate. It was fast alright, but it was also wild and sailed over her catcher's head all the way to the backstop.

"Get down here!" Coach Moore yelled, and Zoe bolted into third base without a throw. She made it, and now the Sting had the winning run on third with two outs.

"Be a tough hitter up there. Hit your shot. Keep battling her!" the Sting's coach shouted to Lily.

Coach Moore then leaned over to Zoe and said, "Get a good jump and be ready for anything."

Zoe, eyes wide, nodded as she adjusted her helmet.

"C'mon Lily. Get me home!"

Now, Natalie was very hot about throwing the wild pitch. Again, she kicked some more dirt up at the back of the pitching circle and muttered under her breath. She kept slamming the softball into her glove. It didn't seem to help calm her as she scrunched her face and panted even faster. She was out of control.

Natalie finally stepped onto the pitching rubber, still talking to herself with a deep-set frown. Without hesitation, she hurtled another fastball towards the plate. This time, the ball was way outside, and the catcher barely got her mitt on it. The softball glanced off her glove and rolled toward the Wildcats' first-base dugout.

"Go, go, go!" Coach Moore yelled, waving her hand.

Zoe took off for home. She could see the catcher scramble towards the now still softball and Natalie sprinting from the circle to cover home plate. Zoe slid, and as she hit the ground, her helmet slipped over her eyes. The catcher fired the ball towards Natalie who was meeting Zoe at the plate at the exact same time. It was going to be close! Zoe felt like time stood still as she slid across the dirt. Still sliding, she felt a hard tag on her left shoulder and a solid jolt on the side of her helmet.

"Safe!" shouted the umpire as he waved his arms. The game was over! The Sting won 3-2!

"Yeah! Yeah!" Zoe screamed as she stood and jumped up and down, the dust falling off her.

The Sting sprinted out of the dugout and mobbed Zoe. A dirt-covered Zoe could do nothing but smile as her teammates hugged her and slapped her on the helmet. Sweat glistened on her forehead, and she smiled as she caught her breath. A voice caught her attention.

"You did it!" Ava yelled, jogging towards Zoe. "You got a clutch hit and then scored the winning run!"

"I couldn't have done it without you, Ava." Zoe blew out her cheeks as a wave of exhaustion hit her.

"You taught me about the reset button and the importance of the pre-pitch routine."

"It was your hard work that paid off, though!" Ava threw her arms around Zoe, squeezing tight. "I just knew you could do it!"

The cheers, fist bumps, and high fives raged on as the Sting rejoiced in their victory. Shrill giggles tore from the girls' lips as they hugged one another, bouncing on the balls of their feet.

Zoe spotted her father who grinned at her. "Great job, Zoe. Way to go!"

"Thanks, Dad!" She waved at both her parents as she headed into the dugout to celebrate with the team.

Grins remained on flushed cheeks as the girls packed up their equipment. Chatter and whoops rang in their ears as the crowd trickled out of Archer Field. Zoe spotted Coach Moore approaching her and Ava from the corner of her eye.

"That was a great game from you two girls." Her face glistened from the afternoon sun and the sweat. Her eyes glimmering with pride. "You've really improved since the first practice, Zoe."

Zoe blushed. "Ava taught me about the importance of the mental game in softball. She taught me that no matter what, the goal is to win the next pitch. You've got to get yourself ready for it. Ava showed me how to deal with my mistakes using a reset and showed me a pre-pitch routine. It sure helped me relax and focus."

Coach Moore grinned. "Mental game skills are just as important as the physical skills. How did you learn about the mental game, Ava?"

"I read a book about the importance of breathing, resetting, and pre-pitch routines. I practiced those things a lot and they really work," Ava said as she tossed her helmet into her bag.

Coach Moore tilted her head, nodding. "I am sure the rest of the girls would love to learn the techniques, too. Could you show them what you've learned?

"That's a great idea!" Zoe grinned at the thought of her team learning more about the mental game of softball.

"Sure thing! Let's do it at our next practice." Ava said with raised eyebrows.

"Sounds like a perfect plan!" Coach Moore said as she hauled the stuffed equipment bag onto her shoulder. The girls bid Coach Moore goodbye as they trudged off the field. Their muscles ached with the game's exertion and their smiles still imprinted on their faces.

"The season is going to be great." Zoe heaved a hopeful sigh.

"Definitely! Hey, we finally got unpacked. Do you want to come over? We can hang out in my new room and watch some videos."

"Sure! That sounds great! I'll ask my mom. I'm sure it will be okay," Zoe said as the girls strolled down the sidewalk. Turning the corner, the sun casting long shadows on the ground around them.

"I know moving is a big change for you, but I am sure glad you moved here!" Zoe said.

"Thanks! Thanks for asking me to play with the Sting and for helping me make new friends. Southport is already feeling like home!" Ava said with a smile.

"Go Sting!" Zoe yelled and the girls giggled.

The Steps of the Reset (Three Ts)

Step 1. Take a Deep Breath

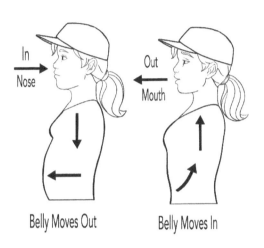

Belly Moves Out

Belly Moves In

Step 2. Throw away the mistake

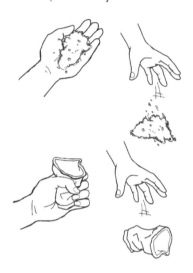

Step 3. Tell Yourself Positive Things

The Steps of the Pre-Pitch Routine

Step 1. Look at Coach

Step 2. Take a Deep Breath

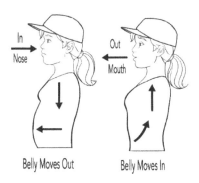

Belly Moves Out   Belly Moves In

Step 3. Study Focal Point

Step 4. Only Look at the Release Point

- Look at the small details of a spot on your bat.
- Really study it
- Don't talk to yourself
- Don't think

Play Better Softball Now!

Write It!

On a sheet of paper, answer the following questions about how you can get ready for the most important pitch in the game—the very next one!

1. In this book, Zoe learned how to use deep breathing to calm herself down when she was nervous. This helped her on the softball field but will also help her in other situations, like when she is nervous about presenting in class or doing something new. She learned a special type of breathing.

   a. What are the three steps for this type of breathing?

   b. When could you use it to help yourself relax while playing softball? When could you use this breathing in other situations?

2. Zoe also learned how important it is to play softball one pitch at a time. This meant that she had to quickly get rid of mistakes so she could focus on the next pitch during a game. Ava called this resetting.

   a. What are the steps (Three Ts) of resetting?

   b. Write down what your reset will look like after you make a mistake in the field.

   c. Write down what you will use as a reset after a bad at bat?

3. Finally, Zoe was too distracted when she batted. She heard everything around her and was always thinking too much when she was in the batter's box. Ava taught her how to use a pre-pitch routine. It was a great way to relax, turn off her thinking, and see the ball right out of the pitcher's hand. This helped Zoe hit better and made her more confident.

   a. What are the steps to a good pre-pitch routine?

b. What will your pre-pitch routine look like? What is the spot on the bat you will look at to turn off your thoughts?

Do It!

4. Practice deep breathing for at least one minute a day every day and notice how it helps you relax.

5. During the day, if you notice yourself feeling anxious or angry, do your deep breathing to calm your body and mind down. Pay attention to how well it works.

6. Practice your pre-pitch routine every day, even when you are not on the softball field. The goal is to get to the point that you aren't thinking anything as you look out at the release point. See how good you can get at doing this!

7. During at least part of your batting practice, imagine that you are playing in a real game. Take your time and do the steps in your pre-pitch routine. Remember, during this type of batting practice, you are turning off all your thoughts and just seeing the ball and hitting it. Don't worry about how hard or where you hit the softball. Just try to get to zero thoughts and

see the ball out of the pitcher's hand all the way to your bat.

8. When you are playing catch with your teammate, take a few throws where you really concentrate on seeing the ball out of her hand. For this drill, turn like you are in the batter's box, take your breath, and focus on your teammate's release point. Try to see the actual spin on the ball. This will train you to see the softball out of her hand when you are at bat.

9. If you miss a ground ball or a pop-up during practice, use the Three Ts to reset. Do this every single time in practice so that it is automatic during games.

10. Teach someone on your team the lessons you have learned in this book. It'll help you remember these skills, and it will also help them become a better softball player too!

I hope you enjoyed the book. You have learned some important skills to help you play better. Practice them in practice so that you will automatically know what to do in a game. Have fun and best of luck!

Doc

Acknowledgements

I'd like to thank the many coaches and players I've worked with over the years. Together, we've exchanged constructive, positive, and usable techniques leading to much success. And, of course, we had a lot of fun along the way!

I'd like to thank those who provided support and suggestions throughout the writing process. I would also like to thank my editor, Olivia Fisher. Her patience and expertise are much appreciated. Her edits improved this book immeasurably.

Finally, I would especially like to thank my wife, Dianne, for her support, patience, and insightful recommendations. Thanks for helping me push through the editing and design decisions to make this book a reality.

Oh, and thank you, too, Oliver!

Acknowledgements

Oliver

140

About the Author

Dr. Curt Ickes is a licensed clinical psychologist who also specializes in sport psychology and has an undying love for baseball and softball. He is fascinated by the application of psychology in sports and teaches techniques that lead to optimal athletic performance. Having taught psychology at Ashland University in Ohio for over three decades (go Eagles!), Dr. Ickes is a professor emeritus at the university and continues his involvement with the AU baseball team. In addition to the Eagles, he works with many other baseball and softball teams. He was also the sport psychologist for the Lake Erie Crushers, a professional baseball team. Curt's first published book, *Mental Toughness: Getting the Edge,* covers sport psychology and mental game skills for more advanced baseball players. His best-selling book, *Win the Next Pitch*, introduces young baseball players ages 8-14 to important mental game skills that build confidence and immediately improve game performance. These books are available on Amazon.com.

Curt hopes his book helps aspiring softball players enjoy the sport even more by teaching them mental game skills and concepts to help them succeed on the field. He also believes that younger athletes can apply these skills in other sports and performance settings. Developing a tough mentality makes children feel more positive about themselves and their teammates. It also helps them understand how best to cope with the inevitable emotions that surround triumph and failure.